Girls

Bible Trivia

50 Extraordinary Quizzes

CONOVER SWOFFORD

SHILOH ♪ kidz
An Imprint of Barbour Publishing, Inc.

© 2020 by Barbour Publishing, Inc.

ISBN 978-1-64352-646-1

All rights reserved. No part of this publication may be reproduced or transmitted for commercial purposes, except for brief quotations in printed reviews, without written permission of the publisher.

Churches and other noncommercial interests may reproduce portions of this book without the express written permission of Barbour Publishing, provided that the text does not exceed 500 words and that the text is not material quoted from another publisher. When reproducing text from this book, include the following credit line: "From *Courageous Girls Bible Trivia*, published by Barbour Publishing, Inc. Used by permission."

Unless otherwise indicated, all scripture quotations are taken from the New Life Version copyright © 1969 and 2003 by Barbour Publishing, Inc. All rights reserved.

Scripture quotations marked KJV are taken from the King James Version of the Bible, with occasional light updating for ease of reading.

Published by Shiloh Kidz, an imprint of Barbour Publishing, Inc., 1810 Barbour Drive, Uhrichsville, Ohio 44683, www.shilohkidz.com

Our mission is to inspire the world with the life-changing message of the Bible.

Member of the
Evangelical Christian
Publishers Association

Printed in the United States of America.

000487 0920 BP

CONTENTS

*Girls, you can change the world
for good. . .when you become the
person God wants you to be.*

This brand-new Bible trivia challenge is based on the popular picture book *100 Extraordinary Stories for Courageous Girls*. It's a fun way to help you learn the scriptures to make yourself and your world better!

Test your knowledge of what the Bible says, and along the way you'll learn a lot about 50 key character traits, including:

- Attitude
- Compassion
- Generosity
- Peacemaking
- Sacrifice
- Work
- and many more

These fun quizzes will show you what God wants for your life—and the lives of the people around you. As a bonus, each quiz also includes a short story about a real woman who changed her world for good. . .for God!

Note: Answers immediately follow each quiz.

AMBITION

(a strong dream, goal, or desire)

In 1927 Charles Lindbergh became the first pilot to fly across the Atlantic Ocean. Americans watched when his plane left New York. They celebrated when it landed in Paris. Later eight-year-old Betty Greene saw Lindbergh in person, and she decided she wanted to be a pilot and have adventures too.

On her sixteenth birthday, Betty received the best gift ever—flying lessons. Her dream to pilot a plane came true, and oh how she loved to fly! She wanted to work as a pilot, but in those days piloting a plane wasn't a common job for women. Her parents encouraged Betty to be a nurse, but that idea didn't interest her. So she followed her dream. Her first job was flying for the American military.

Betty's Christian faith led her to the next step in her flying career. She and three other pilots started an aviation ministry. Their idea was to serve missionaries in other countries. Betty became the Mission Aviation Fellowship's first pilot.

For sixteen years, Betty flew missions for the Lord. What had once seemed her impossible dream had become reality. Betty's story reminds us nothing is impossible for God. If He gives you an ambition, He can make it come true if you let Him.

In the quiz that follows, you will find some people who let God's way and love lead them. . . and some who didn't.

1. A woman named Deborah seems to have had lots of ambition. The Bible says she was what three things?

a. a wife, a prophet, and a judge
b. a prophet, priest, and queen
c. a doctor, lawyer, and carpenter
d. a princess, peacemaker, and priest

2. Jacob wasn't the firstborn, but he still wanted his brother Esau's special firstborn blessing. How did Jacob trick his blind father, Isaac, into giving him Esau's blessing?

a. Jacob dressed like Esau
b. Jacob served his father a special meal
c. Jacob had his mother, Rebekah, help him
d. all the above

3. King David's son Absalom wanted to be king instead of his father. So Absalom started a secret campaign to

a. kill the captain of David's army
b. marry David's wives
c. make all the people like him better than David
d. chase his brothers out of the country

4. When the prophet Samuel anointed Saul king of Israel, Saul

a. said, "Who? Me?"
b. tried to hide
c. yelled, "Yippee!"
d. refused the crown

5. When a rich young man asked Jesus what he could do to inherit eternal life, Jesus told that man that he should give all his money to the poor. The rich young man
  a. did what Jesus told him
  b. ran away and got married
  c. went away sad
  d. laughed at Jesus

6. James and John, two of Jesus' disciples, had their mother ask Jesus to give them important places in His kingdom. The other disciples
  a. thought that was a great idea
  b. got angry with them
  c. asked Jesus for the same favor
  d. quit being Jesus' disciples

7. Nimrod was a mighty hunter who didn't worship God. Nimrod built a famous city that Jonah would later preach in. That city was
  a. Nineveh
  b. Jerusalem
  c. Cairo
  d. New York

✿ ANSWERS ✿

1. a (Judges 4:4)

2. d (Genesis 27:13–19)

3. c (2 Samuel 15:6)

4. b (1 Samuel 10:20–22)

5. c (Mark 10:17–22)

6. b (Matthew 20:20–24)

7. a (Genesis 10:8–11)

ATTITUDE
(the way you think or feel about something or someone)

Fanny Crosby was blind, but she wouldn't allow blindness to make her sad. Instead, she chose to have a positive attitude.

Fanny loved writing poems. She also enjoyed memorizing the Bible, several chapters a week. At age fifteen she left home to attend a school for the blind in New York City.

The New York Institute for the Blind is where Fanny stayed for twenty-three years, not only as a student, but later as a teacher. Everyone around her noticed that Fanny had a talent for writing poetry. Her writing led her to meet famous people, including presidents and governors. She even read one of her poems in the United States Senate chamber in Washington, DC.

Fanny's poems were published in books, but none made her famous. Fame arrived when she began writing lyrics for Sunday school songs and hymns. Soon almost everyone knew her name.

Always she asked God to provide her with ideas for her songs. The ideas came! In her lifetime, Fanny Crosby wrote lyrics for nearly nine thousand songs.

All her life Fanny kept a positive attitude. She even thanked God for her blindness. You can have a positive attitude too if you thank God for everything that happens to you. In the quiz that follows, see what kind of attitudes these people had.

1. In order for Jesus to come to earth to save us from our sins, He had to
a. humble Himself
b. become like a servant
c. look like a man
d. all the above

2. When Mary sat at Jesus' feet, just listening to Him, Jesus told her sister Martha that Mary's attitude was good. According to Jesus, Mary
a. was lazy
b. had chosen what was most important
c. should be yelled at
d. would go help Martha

3. Jesus once called James and John the "Sons of Thunder," apparently because they were angry. That was when they asked Jesus if they could call down fire on a village that
a. laughed at them
b. wouldn't welcome Jesus
c. kept an idol in the town square
d. smelled like old fish

4. Jesus told a parable about a judge who was mean to a woman. Jesus said the judge was mean because
a. he didn't fear God
b. he just liked being mean
c. he was born that way
d. other people were mean to him

5. Ahab was the nastiest king Israel ever had. The Bible says that no one before Ahab did more _____ in the eyes of the Lord.

    a. stupid stuff
    b. damage
    c. sin and evil
    d. destruction

6. Jesus told a parable about a Pharisee and a tax collector who went to the temple to pray. The Pharisee was proud and selfish and prayed about

    a. himself
    b. the tax collector
    c. the Jews
    d. his dog

7. In the same parable, the tax collector worshipped God and prayed

    a. loudly
    b. that God would pity him
    c. for his wife
    d. for the Pharisee

❀ ANSWERS ❀

1. d (Philippians 2:7-8)

2. b (Luke 10:42)

3. b (Luke 9:51-56. Of course, Jesus wouldn't let them do it!)

4. a (Luke 18:1-8)

5. c (1 Kings 16:30)

6. a (Luke 18:11)

7. b (Luke 18:13)

BELIEF

(the trust you have in a person, thing, or idea)

In old-time England, some kings and queens came to power in sneaky ways. The 1500s were a time when Protestants and Catholics disagreed strongly about their beliefs. Some of them even killed each other.

A woman named Jane was born into a royal family. When she was old enough, her dad arranged her marriage to a nobleman. Lady Jane's cousin Edward, who would become King Edward VI, had a half-sister named Mary. All this is important because Jane, her dad, her husband, and Edward were all Protestants. Edward's sister, Mary, was Catholic.

When Edward was ten, he became king. But he was a sickly boy, and he died at fifteen. Before that, Edward made Jane queen. But she reigned only nine days. Edward's half sister Mary managed to convince others in power that *she* should be queen instead of Jane.

Mary and Jane strongly disagreed over whose religious beliefs were right. When Jane spoke out against what the queen believed, Mary ordered that she be killed.

As Jane awaited her execution, she refused to deny her beliefs. Just before she was killed, Jane quoted Jesus' words from the cross: "Father, into Your hands I give My spirit" (Luke 23:46). She trusted God to the very end.

Belief in God is important. Here are some biblical examples to help you grow that belief.

1. God promised Abraham that he would have a son and his descendants would one day live in the "Promised Land." What did God say Abraham's belief counted as?

    a. total success

    b. victory

    c. being right with God

    d. solid gold

2. When an angel came to tell Mary that she would give birth to the Son of God, her belief in the Lord was so strong that she said to the angel:

    a. "Let it happen to me as you have said."

    b. "I hope God knows what He's doing."

    c. "I am willing to be used of the Lord."

    d. a and c

3. Jesus asked two blind men if they believed He could heal them. They said, "Yes, Sir!" and Jesus

    a. walked away

    b. healed them

    c. laughed

    d. told them to see the priest

4. The Israelites wandered in the wilderness for forty years because they didn't believe God would give them the Promised Land. Why didn't they believe what God had said?

    a. they were afraid of the people who
       already lived in the land

    b. they hated Moses

    c. Aaron told them lies about God

    d. they were distracted by grasshoppers

5. The New Testament believers came together to worship and fellowship and they
a. believed in the apostles' teachings
b. spent time together daily
c. shared all their possessions
d. all the above

6. God so loved the world that He gave His one and only Son that whoever believes in Him
a. shall not perish
b. shall have eternal life
c. shall get rich
d. a and b

7. The Bible says that anyone who comes to God must believe that
a. God exists
b. God is nice
c. God wants to punish them
d. God knows everything

❀ ANSWERS ❀

1. c (Genesis 15:6)

2. d (Luke 1:38)

3. b (Matthew 9:27–29)

4. a (Numbers 13:31)

5. d (Acts 2:42–47)

6. d (John 3:16)

7. a (Hebrews 11:6)

CALLING

(a strong desire to a certain way of life or job)

Huldah's is another small story in the Bible. Not much is written about her, but what she did was life changing.

Huldah lived during the reign of Judah's King Josiah, a good king who loved God. He became king following years—generations—of bad kings. Josiah was only eight when he took the throne and eighteen when he discovered something great—a scroll containing God's laws, the ones He'd given to Moses many years before.

Huldah, wife of the king's wardrobe keeper, had a calling. She was a prophetess—a woman with the gift of talking with God and passing His words on to the people. King Josiah sent his men to her to ask what God had to say to the people. Josiah knew Israel had disobeyed God's law.

Huldah said God was angry with His people for the things they had done. The Book of the Law said God would punish His people for disobeying. But when Huldah talked with God, He told her He was pleased with Josiah. God promised to hold off His punishment as long as Josiah lived. The king's men carried God's message back to the king, and Josiah believed what Huldah said.

God had given Huldah a perfect calling. In the following quizzes, let's see what you know about the callings of other Bible characters.

1. More than one woman is named in the Bible as a prophet. Besides Huldah, who else had that calling?
   a. Deborah
   b. Miriam
   c. Zilpah
   d. a and b above

2. Before he was born, an angel told the John the Baptist's father that his son had a calling from God to
   a. get people ready for the Lord
   b. sing and dance
   c. write important books
   d. yell at the people

3. Jesus called Peter and Andrew to be His disciples while they were
   a. hunting
   b. cooking
   c. eating
   d. fishing

4. The book of 2 Peter says that Christians are to make our calling sure so that we will never
   a. fear
   b. fall
   c. cheat
   d. sin

5. God called Moses to lead the children of Israel out of Egypt. God got Moses' attention by showing him
a. a singing sheep
b. a burning bush
c. a glowing cloud
d. a towering mountain

6. When God first called Abraham, He asked Abraham to
a. become a farmer
b. marry Ruth
c. tend God's sheep
d. move to another country

7. God called to the prophet Samuel in the night while Samuel was
a. reading
b. eating
c. lying down
d. praying

✿ ANSWERS ✿

1. d (Judges 4:4; Exodus 15:20)

2. a (Luke 1:17)

3. d (Matthew 4:18-20)

4. b (2 Peter 1:10)

5. b (Exodus 3:2)

6. d (Genesis 12:1)

7. c (1 Samuel 3:3-4)

CHARACTER

(being good; doing the right thing)

In the mid-1950s in Montgomery, Alabama, where Rosa Parks lived, many laws separated African-Americans from white people. This was wrong. Many knew it, but Rosa Parks did something about it.

Buses had assigned seats, meaning that white people sat in the front half of the bus and African-Americans in the back. A sign in the aisle separated the races.

One day Rosa sat near the middle of the bus in one of the first rows assigned to African-Americans. The bus driver told the African-Americans in their front rows to stand up and move back so the white passengers could sit. Rosa had spent her life being told she wasn't good enough to sit in the front of the bus and do other things white people did, so Rosa said, "No." The driver called the police, and they arrested Rosa.

African-Americans in Montgomery decided to boycott the buses—that meant they wouldn't ride on them. They also got African-American leaders like Martin Luther King Jr. involved in working to change the law. The boycott lasted almost a year, and it was a huge success. The law changed so everyone could sit anywhere on the buses. Rosa showed good character.

Bible people had both good and bad character. Let's see if you remember some things about the kind of character God wants *you* to have.

1. Who did King Darius's law say everyone needed to pray to?
   a. King Darius
   b. idols
   c. a statue
   d. themselves

2. According to the Proverbs, the woman of noble character will have children who do what?
   a. honor her
   b. live long lives
   c. clean their rooms
   d. send her flowers

3. Although David knew that he would someday be king, how did he respond when King Saul tried to kill him?
   a. David refused to try to kill King Saul
   b. David ignored King Saul
   c. David didn't believe King Saul was trying to kill him
   d. David took a long ocean cruise

4. Barnabas—who sold a field and gave the money to help poor Christians—was nicknamed
   a. Son of Generosity
   b. Son of Comfort
   c. Son of Silver
   d. Sonny

5. Jesus said that to enter the kingdom of heaven you must become like little
   a. ants
   b. children
   c. monsters
   d. men

6. Elisha's servant, Gehazi, showed bad character by lying to Naaman to get silver and valuable robes. What was Gehazi's punishment?
   a. he was beaten
   b. he was put in prison
   c. he got Naaman's bad skin disease
   d. he was severely scolded

7. Samson was strong in body but weak in character. What did he let Delilah do that made his strength disappear?
   a. kiss him
   b. hold his hand
   c. cut his hair
   d. cook him broccoli

❧ ANSWERS ❧

1. a (Daniel 6:7-9)

2. a (Proverbs 31:28)

3. a (1 Samuel 24:10)

4. b (Acts 4:36-37)

5. b (Matthew 18:3)

6. c (2 Kings 5:26-27)

7. c (Judges 16:18-19)

➤ QUIZ 6 ➤
CHEERFULNESS
(being happy)

Anne Steele was a British songwriter and poet in the 1700s. Life wasn't easy for her, but she always did her best to have a cheerful attitude.

Anne's mom died when Anne was just three years old. When Anne was a teenager, she got malaria and suffered from it for the rest of her life. Still, Anne chose to look on the bright side. She often entertained her friends by reading them poems she had written. Her poems were good—good enough to be set to music and shared with the world. But "Nanny," as her friends and family called her, was not eager to publish them. She was humble, not wanting to draw attention to herself. Anne would be in her forties before she agreed to share her work with others

Anne finally published her poetry and essays using a pen name, Theodosia, and she gave the money she earned to charities. The hymns she wrote became very popular, especially in Baptist churches. She wrote 144 hymns, many poems and essays, and became known as "the mother of the English hymn." Some of Anne's hymns are included in hymnals still used in churches today.

God can accomplish a lot in you if you have a cheerful attitude. See what the Bible says about cheerfulness.

1. The Bible tells us to give to God cheerfully because He _____ a cheerful giver.
   a. blesses
   b. loves
   c. empowers
   d. throws a party for

2. The Proverbs say that a glad heart makes your _____ happy.
   a. body
   b. friends
   c. face
   d. parents

3. The Proverbs also say a glad heart is as good for your body as
   a. behaving in school
   b. winning a race
   c. talking to your friends
   d. taking medicine

4. When you are cheerful, chances are you find it easier to laugh. What happened to Sarah to make her say, "God has made me laugh. All who hear will laugh with me"?
   a. She got a raise in pay.
   b. She found a coin she had lost.
   c. She had a newborn baby boy.
   d. She bought a new outfit.

5. Why did Jesus say every Christian should "be of good cheer"?

a. "I have overcome the world."
b. "You are going to heaven."
c. "God owns the cattle on a thousand hills."
d. "There will never be another great flood."

6. According to the book of Ecclesiastes, when should people be most cheerful?

a. when they're young
b. when they're middle aged
c. when they're old
d. when they're dead

7. According to the Psalms, when you make yourself happy in the Lord, what do you get?

a. chocolate ice cream
b. money and health
c. unending sunshine
d. the desires of your heart

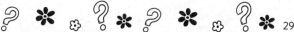

❁ ANSWERS ❁

1. b (2 Corinthians 9:7 KJV)

2. c (Proverbs 15:13)

3. d (Proverbs 17:22)

4. c (Genesis 21:2-7)

5. a (John 16:33 KJV)

6. a (Ecclesiastes 11:9)

7. d (Psalm 37:4)

✦ QUIZ 7 ✦
COMPASSION
(loving-kindness)

In Bible times, Naaman, a leader of the Syrian army, had an awful skin disease. Could anyone heal him?

Syrian soldiers had raided a home and kidnapped a young Jewish girl. She became a servant to Naaman's wife. The Bible doesn't mention her name, but we know she loved God and also that she trusted Elisha, one of God's prophets in Israel. When the girl saw how miserable Naaman was, she told his wife, "I wish that my owner's husband were with the man of God who is in Samaria! Then he would heal his bad skin disease" (2 Kings 5:3).

Naaman didn't believe in the one true God, but he was ready to try anything. He went to Elisha. Naaman was told to wash in the dirty Jordan River seven times. He did and he was healed! He understood then the power of the one and only God. From that day on, Naaman became a believer—thanks to a servant girl who bravely shared her trust in God's power.

If someone you know has trouble, even if it's someone who has been mean to you, you can be like the servant girl and have compassion on that person. You can remind them that God can do anything.

Let's look at how some other people showed God's compassion to others.

1. Who showed compassion to a widow named Ruth by letting her glean (pick up the leftovers) in his field?
   a. Boaz
   b. Jesus
   c. Paul
   d. Peter

2. In Jesus' story of a stranger who took compassion on a man who had been robbed and beaten up, Jesus said this good stranger was a
   a. Jew
   b. Ninevite
   c. Samaritan
   d. Russian

3. When a lame beggar asked Peter and John for money, how did Peter show the man compassion?
   a. He gave him a drink of water
   b. He healed him so he could walk
   c. He patted him gently on the head
   d. He gave him two dollars

4. Jesus had compassion on two sisters by raising their brother, Lazarus, from the dead. Who were the sisters?
   a. Rachel and Leah
   b. Jezebel and Athaliah
   c. Anna and Huldah
   d. Mary and Martha

5. The Bible says that God shows His compassion to people
   a. every morning
   b. when the sun is shining
   c. only on Sundays
   d. every third Christmas

6. When two blind men asked Jesus to have compassion on them, Jesus
   a. gave them money
   b. healed them so they could see
   c. sent them to the temple
   d. told them to come back in a week

7. When Jesus showed compassion on a demon-possessed man, He sent the demons into a herd of
   a. pigs
   b. deer
   c. cows
   d. cats

❁ ANSWERS ❁

1. a (Ruth 2:8–9)

2. c (Luke 10:33)

3. b (Acts 3:7–8)

4. d (John 11:1)

5. a (Lamentations 3:23)

6. b (Matthew 9:27–30)

7. a (Mark 5:1–13)

❧ QUIZ 8 ❧
COURAGE
(bravery)

In Bible times, Deborah was Israel's only female judge. She was a fair judge who trusted God. And God trusted Deborah with a dangerous mission: to free the Israelites from the control of Canaan's cruel King Jabin.

The king's gigantic army with its nine hundred chariots terrified the Israelites. They suffered under the king's rule. God didn't want that. He wanted His people freed from Jabin's evil ways.

God often spoke through Deborah to the people of Israel. One day He gave her a message for a man named Barak: "Take with you 10,000 men. . . . I will have Sisera, the head of Jabin's army, meet you. . . . I will give him into your hand." (Judges 4:6–7).

But Barak was afraid. "I will go if you go with me," he told Deborah (verse 8).

"I will go with you," she answered bravely. "But the honor will not be yours as you go on your way. For the Lord will sell Sisera into the hands of a woman" (verse 9).

Deborah faced danger to keep the Israelites safe from a bad king.

Are you brave like Deborah? Whenever you need courage, ask God. He will help you. Let's see how God gave some other people the courage to do what is right.

1. The Jewish priests put Peter and John in jail for preaching about Jesus. When Peter and John got out of jail
    a. they told the priests nothing could stop them from preaching
    b. they ran away and hid
    c. they left Jerusalem
    d. none of the above

2. When Joshua sent two spies into Jericho, Rahab hid the spies from the king because
    a. she hated the king
    b. she believed in God's power
    c. Joshua told her to
    d. the spies made her

3. When Daniel was told that he could only pray to King Darius, Daniel
    a. prayed only to King Darius
    b. didn't pray at all
    c. continued to pray to God three times a day
    d. hid under his bed

4. Anyone trying to see the king without his invitation could be put to death. But Esther knew that to save her people, she had to try. When Esther went to see the king
    a. his bodyguards stopped her
    b. he made her leave the kingdom
    c. he had her put to death
    d. he held out his scepter

5. After Elijah ran away from the wicked Queen Jezebel, God gave Elijah the courage to
a. apologize to her
b. shoot her with an arrow
c. go back the way he'd come
d. be a spy in her palace

6. Because Stephen, an early Christian, told the Jews about Jesus, the Jews
a. accepted Jesus
b. stoned Stephen to death
c. ignored him
d. put him in jail

7. Even though Paul knew he would be arrested if he went to Jerusalem to preach about Jesus, Paul
a. went anyway
b. hid
c. ran away
d. went sailing

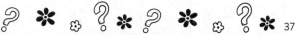

✿ ANSWERS ✿

1. a (Acts 4:19–20)

2. c (Daniel 6:10)

3. c (Daniel 6:10)

4. d (Esther 5:2)

5. c (1 Kings 19:15–19)

6. b (Acts 7:59)

7. a (Acts 21:10–17)

QUIZ 9
CURIOSITY
(wanting to know something)

When God created the earth, He made everything to be very good. God put all kinds of beautiful trees with delicious fruit there. At the center of the garden, He set a special tree, the tree of learning about good and evil. God didn't want Adam to know about evil things, so He ordered Adam never to eat fruit from that tree. Next, God created a perfect woman as a helper for Adam. She was Eve.

Eve felt curious about that center tree in the garden. She was even more curious when a sneaky snake told her that eating fruit from the tree would make her like God, knowing both good and evil. The Bible says, "The woman saw that the tree was good for food, and pleasing to the eyes, and could fill the desire of making one wise. So she took of its fruit and ate. She also gave some to her husband, and he ate" (Genesis 3:6)

It was the worst mistake ever! Eating that fruit opened their eyes to everything evil and allowed sin to enter the world. Eve's mistake—disobeying God—changed the world forever. Eve's mistake reminds us to obey God and do what is right. You can't allow your curiosity about something to overcome your obedience to God.

What can you learn from the curiosity of these Bible people?

1. What kind of fruit grew on the tree that Eve and Adam ate from?
   a. apple
   b. pear
   c. watermelon
   d. the Bible doesn't say

2. Moses was tending to a flock of sheep when a curious sight caught his eye. Moses saw
   a. his brother, Aaron
   b. another flock of sheep
   c. a burning bush
   d. a glowing angel

3. When Jesus talked about water to the Samaritan woman at the well, she was curious to know
   a. how Jesus could get water from the well
   b. how the water Jesus spoke of would keep someone from becoming thirsty again
   c. if Jesus was the One called the Christ
   d. all the above

4. Simon the Sorcerer saw believers in Jesus receiving the Holy Spirit after Peter and John laid their hands on them. Simon thought it was a magic trick and tried to get Peter and John to
   a. stop doing it
   b. go away
   c. sing and dance
   d. sell it to him

5. Jesus told the story of the Good Samaritan because someone asked Jesus
   a. What's good about a Samaritan?
   b. How can I be saved?
   c. Who is my neighbor?
   d. Where are you going?

6. When some men of Bethshemesh looked into the Ark of the Covenant when they weren't supposed to, God
   a. struck them dead
   b. gave them leprosy
   c. blessed them
   d. turned them into a pillar of salt

7. When an earthquake opened the prison doors for Paul and Silas, the jailer asked them
   a. Is this your fault?
   b. Is everyone alive?
   c. What must I do to be saved?
   d. Do you want a lawyer?

✿ ANSWERS ✿

1. d (Genesis 3:6)

2. c (Exodus 3:1-3)

3. d (John 4:11-26)

4. d (Acts 8:18)

5. c (Luke 10:29)

6. a (1 Samuel 6:19. God had already warned the people very strongly against doing this.)

7. c (Acts 16:30)

DEDICATION

(being faithful or devoted to something)

As a young girl growing up in England, Elizabeth Fry had no idea what it was like being poor. Her father, a banker, gave his children everything they needed and more.

Elizabeth had a kind heart and concern for the poor. When she was in her teens, Elizabeth compared her life to theirs, and she wondered if God existed. God knew what she was thinking! He put the idea in Elizabeth's heart to do something to help.

Elizabeth began by making clothes for poor people. She started a Sunday school for them and taught them to read.

God had a plan for her. He led her to visit a women's prison, and when Elizabeth saw the filthy, terrible place, she found her purpose. She became like an angel to the women there. She prayed for and with them, and she taught them to get along and to be fair to one another. When they wanted to set up a school in prison, Elizabeth helped make it happen.

Elizabeth was strong about her opinions. She never gave up. She stood up to those who were against her, and she got things done. What can you learn from these Biblical examples of dedication to God and what God wants you to do?

1. Solomon made a sacrifice of 22,000 cattle and 120,000 sheep when he dedicated
   a. his palace
   b. a new bridge
   c. the house of the Lord
   d. his first son

2. Who told Samson's parents before Samson was born that he was to be a Nazarite, a person dedicated to the Lord?
   a. Samson's grandparents
   b. a talking donkey
   c. a prophet
   d. an angel

3. When Mary and Joseph took the baby Jesus to the temple to dedicate Him to the Lord, they had to
   a. offer a sacrifice
   b. pay taxes
   c. hide Jesus from the Roman soldiers
   d. tell their parents

4. When Abraham arrived in the land God had led him to, he dedicated that land to God by building _____ to the Lord.
   a. a tower
   b. a temple
   c. an altar
   d. a statue

5. Joshua was the dedicated follower of Moses. After Moses died, God made Joshua
a. the leader of Israel
b. wear Moses' coat
c. go to Egypt
d. carry Moses' bones

6. Esther risked her life by going uninvited to see the king because she was dedicated to
a. keeping her good looks
b. saving her people
c. being queen
d. killing Mordecai

7. In order to stay with Naomi, Ruth dedicated herself to Naomi, Naomi's people, and Naomi's
a. health
b. boyfriend
c. well-being
d. God

✿ ANSWERS ✿

1. c (1 Kings 8:62-63)

2. d (Judges 13:2-5)

3. a (Luke 2:22-24)

4. c (Genesis 12:8)

5. a (Joshua 1:1-2)

6. b (Esther 4:13-16)

7. d (Ruth 1:16)

DILIGENCE
(careful and continual effort)

Elizabeth Prentiss grew up a sickly little girl. She once said she had never known what it feels like to be well. Elizabeth suffered from pain in her side, fainting spells, and headaches that upset her stomach. Every day something made her unwell. Her illnesses caused Elizabeth to feel gloomy, but she wore a happy face anyway. She put all her strength into living, and those around her saw a cheery girl with a sense of humor.

God gave Elizabeth Prentiss a special talent—writing. Her mom understood that Elizabeth needed a quiet space where she could think and write. So she set up a special room in their house where Elizabeth could work.

As she wrote, Elizabeth discovered that she loved writing for kids. Some of her first stories and poems were published when Elizabeth was just sixteen. Because she was Christian and loved God, Elizabeth wrote stories that she hoped would lead children—and adults too—to "do good." She found inspiration for her stories, poems, and songs in even the most difficult times of her life.

Elizabeth was diligent in using her talent to serve God. See what you can learn from these examples of diligence.

1. Jesus went about doing good because
   a. God anointed Him with the Holy Spirit
   b. God was with Him
   c. Jesus was setting a good example
   d. all the above

2. The book of Proverbs says that lazy hands make a man poor, but diligent (or steady or hardworking) hands bring
   a. warts
   b. wealth
   c. anger
   d. friendship

3. When the children of Israel returned from captivity, they had to rebuild the city of Jerusalem. Ezra told them to be especially diligent to rebuild
   a. their houses
   b. their barns
   c. the temple—God's house
   d. their playgrounds

4. When Laban tricked Jacob by giving him Leah as his wife, Jacob diligently worked for Laban another seven years so he could have Leah's sister, _____, as his wife too.
   a. Ruth
   b. Naomi
   c. Rachel
   d. Esther

5. The apostle Paul was diligent about preaching the Gospel of Jesus. Even when he was in prison in Rome, he preached to

   a. his mom
   b. everyone who visited
   c. the emperor
   d. the garbage collector

6. Because the prophet Jeremiah was diligent to tell the Israelites God's message, the king of Judah

   a. threw Jeremiah into prison
   b. told him to stop talking or die
   c. finally listened
   d. a and b

7. When Samuel came to anoint David to be king of Israel, David was diligently tending to his father's

   a. sheep
   b. goats
   c. vineyards
   d. horses

❀ ANSWERS ❀

1. d (Acts 10:38; John 1:1; 13:15)

2. b (Proverbs 10:4)

3. c (Ezra 7:23)

4. c (Genesis 29:26–28)

5. b (Acts 28:30–31)

6. d (Jeremiah 37:18; 38:24)

7. a (1 Samuel 16:11–13)

DUTY

(things a person should or must do)

Queen Esther kept a secret from her husband: she was Jewish.

Esther's cousin, Mordecai, kept her secret by pretending that he and Esther, who he had raised, weren't related. But he often hung around the castle gate to get a glimpse of Esther to be sure she was okay.

One day an evil man named Haman ordered Mordecai to bow to him, but Mordecai refused. He would bow only to God. That made Haman angry. He went to the king. "Jews are terrible people," Haman said. He convinced the king to order that all the Jews be killed. Mordecai got a message to Esther. He told her what was going on.

I have to tell my husband that I'm Jewish, Esther thought. *I must convince him not to kill the Jewish people.* She sent Mordecai a message: "Pray for me. I will go in to the king, which is against the law. And if I die, I die."

It was a scary thing, but Esther confessed the truth to the king. The king's attitude about murdering the Jews changed. All their lives were spared, thanks to Esther telling the truth.

Like Esther, part of your duty to God is to tell the truth. When you do, you can be sure God is on your side.

Now let's check out how other people did with their God-given duties!

1. Hezekiah was one of the best kings Judah ever had. When Hezekiah became king, the people of Judah were worshipping false gods. So Hezekiah did his duty and
   a. repaired the temple
   b. celebrated Passover
   c. tore down all the places where false gods were worshipped
   d. all the above

2. Before he became a Christian, Saul (who later became Paul) thought he was doing his duty to God by
   a. hurting the church
   b. shaving his head
   c. burning Bibles
   d. giving up wine

3. Because he was the nearest relative by law, it was Boaz's duty to marry
   a. Mary
   b. Ruth
   c. Martha
   d. Naomi

4. God gave Jonah the duty of preaching to the city of Nineveh but Jonah
   a. ran away
   b. pretended he didn't hear God
   c. locked himself in his bedroom
   d. asked a friend to go instead

5. Jesus dutifully came to earth and died on the cross
a. to save us from our sins
b. because He loves us
c. in obedience to His Father
d. all the above

6. In Acts there are several mentions of a man named Barnabas who helped the disciples by
a. selling a field and bringing them the money
b. bringing Paul to them
c. going on a missionary journey with Paul
d. all the above

7. When Joseph, the husband of Mary, found out that Mary was expecting a child, he
a. broke up with her
b. married her
c. married her sister
d. ran away

✿ ANSWERS ✿

1. d (2 Chronicles 29–31)

2. a (Acts 8:3. Obviously, Saul was mistaken!)

3. b (Ruth 4:1–10)

4. a (Jonah 1:2–3)

5. d (Matthew 1:21; Romans 5:8;
   Matthew 26:39)

6. d (Acts 4:37; 9:27; 13:2–4)

7. b (Matthew 1:18–24)

⇒ QUIZ 13 ⇐

ENDURANCE

(sticking with something no matter what)

Anne Marbury grew up in England when the Church of England ruled and the Puritans rebelled. Her parents taught her to think for herself.

When Anne was older, she married William Hutchinson. The couple enjoyed listening to a Puritan minister, John Cotton. The Church of England disliked John for his teachings, so John moved to the Massachusetts Bay Colony in America. Anne and William followed him. They thought everyone in the colony would have complete freedom to believe and worship as they pleased. That wasn't what happened.

The colony's governor, John Winthrop, wanted everyone to follow strict Puritan rules. That meant women were to keep their beliefs to themselves and allow the men to lead. But Anne held meetings in her house where people could discuss religion and that upset Governor Winthrop.

He claimed it wasn't right for a woman to teach men, and he put Anne on trial for teaching something that was against what the church believed. At her trial, Anne answered the governor's questions by quoting Bible verses. Winthrop found Anne's answers disrespectful. The rulers found Anne guilty and kicked her out of the colony!

It was women like Anne who gave American women courage to speak up and fight for what they believe. It takes endurance to stick to what you know is right. What can you learn about endurance from this quiz?

1. When the Israelites fought the Amalekites, as long as Moses raised his hands to God, the Israelites won. But when Moses got tired and had to lower his hands, the Amalekites won. So when Moses had trouble holding up his hands
   a. Aaron and Hur held them up for him
   b. the Amalekites claimed total victory
   c. Moses passed out
   d. he got a frozen shoulder

2. The book of Hebrews says we are to run with endurance the race God has marked out for us. That race is a symbol for
   a. how we live our Christian lives
   b. the Olympics
   c. preaching
   d. raising a family

3. When Paul and Silas were beaten and thrown into prison in Philippi, they endured their hardship by
   a. telling jokes
   b. thinking good thoughts
   c. praying and singing hymns to God
   d. making friends with other prisoners

4. The psalm writer says he can endure the valley of the shadow of death because
   a. he's not afraid of anything
   b. God is with him
   c. he has friends
   d. he's heading for the mountain of light

5. Jesus endured all the horror of being crucified on the cross
   a. for the joy of being with God later
   b. because He loves us
   c. because He's the only one who could save us from our sins
   d. all the above

6. Although King Saul hunted David and tried to kill him, David endured it and didn't try to harm King Saul in any way because
   a. King Saul was the Lord's chosen king
   b. David was afraid of King Saul
   c. King Saul was David's master
   d. Saul would later become the Christian Paul

7. Deborah, the only female judge of Israel, was told by God to command Barak to go fight the Canaanites. But Barak couldn't endure the idea and said he would only go if
   a. his mom could come with him
   b. Deborah went with him
   c. he could wear the king's armor
   d. he heard the command directly from God

❀ ANSWERS ❀

1. a (Exodus 17:8–13)

2. a (Hebrews 12:1)

3. c (Acts 16:25)

4. b (Psalm 23:4)

5. d (Hebrews 12:2; Romans 5:8; Acts 4:12)

6. a (1 Samuel 24:6)

7. b (Judges 4:8)

FAITHFULNESS

(loyalty to something or someone)

Imagine yourself living in Jerusalem in the years before Jesus' birth. Whenever you entered the temple to pray, you would see Anna. The old woman almost never left the temple. She stayed there day and night praying, sometimes going without food so she could pray even better.

Anna spent most of her life learning God's Word and talking with Him in prayer. She had married as a young woman and lived with her husband for only seven years until he died. Anna remained single the rest of her life, and she turned her attention toward God. She believed with her whole heart what the scriptures said about a Messiah coming to save the world from sin. Anna waited for Him to arrive. Year after year she waited patiently, never doubting.

When Anna was very old, Mary and Joseph brought Jesus to the temple to dedicate Him to God. The Spirit of God had promised a man named Simeon that he would not die until he saw the Messiah with his own eyes, and now Simeon held baby Jesus, the Messiah. And Anna was right there with him!

Anna's faith was rewarded. She went out and told the people in Jerusalem about Jesus. Anna became the first woman ever to share the Good News about Jesus' birth.

How can you learn to be faithful? By following these Bible examples:

1. Cornelius was faithful to God even though he was not Jewish. Cornelius was
   a. a Roman "centurion," or army captain
   b. the king of another nation
   c. a Roman tax collector
   d. a slave in Pilate's household

2. The book of Romans says that faith comes from
   a. praying every day
   b. hearing the Gospel message
   c. telling others about Jesus
   d. obeying your parents

3. Baby Moses' parents showed their faith by
   a. praying in public
   b. holding worship services at their house
   c. not fearing Pharaoh's threat to kill Hebrew babies
   d. telling their friends about God

4. What city did God say Joshua would defeat if he faithfully marched around it for seven days?
   a. Jerusalem
   b. Nineveh
   c. Bethlehem
   d. Jericho

5. Because Solomon had faith in God, he asked God for
a. love
b. wisdom
c. money
d. a wife

6. What did faithful Ruth tell her widowed mother-in-law, Naomi, as Naomi planned to return to Jerusalem?
a. "I will go where you go"
b. "I will live where you live"
c. "Your God will be my God"
d. all the above

7. Faithful Deborah believed God when He said He would give Israel victory over their enemy Sisera. Because Israel's commander Barak did not, Deborah told him,
a. "The Lord will sell Sisera into the hands of a woman."
b. "Your chariot will get stuck in the mud."
c. "Oh you of little faith. Why do you not believe?"
d. "Just do it! And God will reward you."

❀ ANSWERS ❀

1. a (Acts 10:1)

2. b (Romans 10:17)

3. c (Hebrews 11:23)

4. d (Hebrews 11:30)

5. b (1 Kings 3:9–12)

6. d (Ruth 1:16)

7. a (Judges 4:9)

FRIENDSHIP

(being a buddy)

Do you like to write? Esther Burr did. In a time long before computers made writing easy, Esther journaled and wrote letters. Although she lived almost three hundred years ago, her letters and journals still exist. From reading them, we can learn about true friendship.

Esther's best friend, Sarah, lived too far away to visit in person. There were no cars, planes, or trains then. People relied on horses, and travel took a long time. The two women wrote letters to each other.

Her friendship with Sarah, according to Esther, was a gift from God, one that would last forever. In her journal, Esther said it this way: "True friendship is first inkindled by a spark from heaven, and heaven will never suffer it to go out, but it will burn to all eternity."

When Esther didn't have a friend in her town who would talk with her about Jesus, she knew she could write about Him to Sarah. Both were Christians who loved the Lord, and they openly shared their faith with each other. The two friends wrote more than a hundred letters before Esther died of a fever at the young age of age twenty-six.

Let's see what more the Bible can teach you—and your friends—about friendship!

1. How does the Bible say Jonathan loved David?
   a. as he loved himself
   b. as high as the heavens are above the earth
   c. as deep as the ocean
   d. as much as he loved video games

2. Who were Jesus' closest friends among the twelve disciples?
   a. Judas, Judas Iscariot, and Simon the Canaanite
   b. Peter, James, and John
   c. Philip, Bartholomew, and Thomas
   d. Andrew, Matthew, and James, the son of Alphaeus

3. According to the Proverbs, when does a friend love you?
   a. only in good weather
   b. when he agrees with you
   c. all the time
   d. every third Sunday

4. What did the three friends Shadrach, Meshach, and Abednego do to get themselves thrown into a fiery furnace?
   a. write on the bathroom wall
   b. refuse to bow before a golden statue
   c. forget the king's birthday
   d. preach to the Ninevites

5. When Judas betrayed Jesus with a kiss, Jesus said, "Friend. . .
   a. watch your step"
   b. do what you came to do"
   c. are you sure you want to do this?"
   d. get your lips off me"

6. Abraham was called the friend of
   a. Jesus
   b. Judas
   c. Lot
   d. God

7. Some people tried to disrespect Jesus by saying He was not only a friend of sinners but also of
   a. drunks
   b. overeaters
   c. tax collectors
   d. all of the above

❀ ANSWERS ❀

1. a (1 Samuel 18:3)

2. b (Matthew 17:1; Mark 14:33; Luke 9:28)

3. c (Proverbs 17:17)

4. b (Daniel 3)

5. b (Matthew 26:50)

6. d (James 2:23)

7. d (Matthew 11:19)

≽ QUIZ 16 ≼
GENEROSITY
(showing you're ready and willing to give)

Do you know a kid who lives with someone other than their parents? Mary Jane Kinnaird's parents died when she was little. Her grandpa, older brother, and aunts and uncles raised her in England. Mary Jane's family was blessed with money, so she had a governess too.

Bible study was important to Mary Jane. Her uncle was a minister, and when Mary Jane was older, she became his secretary. At the same time, she began making plans to help others. Surely her family had enough money to be generous.

Mary Jane later married a wealthy man named Arthur Kinnaird. Together they raised money for many good causes.

Mary Jane's first project was a training school for servants who worked doing chores like cooking, laundry, and cleaning for others.

That led to something wonderful. Mary Jane made it grow until it became four schools. Then she combined it with a Bible study group. The organization became the Young Women's Christian Association—the YWCA!

Today the YWCA helps women and girls from all backgrounds become the best they can be. It promotes leadership and the idea that everyone is equal.

Mary Jane helped others with her money, but there are other ways to be generous.

What can you learn about generosity from the people in this quiz?

1. When a rich young man asked Jesus what he must do to inherit eternal life, what did Jesus tell him?
   a. sell everything and give the money to the poor
   b. buy your parents a nice house
   c. sponsor a missionary
   d. build a church

2. After the tax collector Zaccheus met Jesus, how much of his money did he promise to give to the poor?
   a. all of it
   b. one tenth
   c. half of it
   d. not a penny

3. When a lame beggar asked Peter and John for money, Peter told him, "I have something better I can give you in the name of Jesus Christ." Then Peter
   a. handed him a Bible
   b. smiled warmly
   c. took him by the hand, helped him up, and healed him
   d. gave him new crutches

4. When God showed Abraham's servant that Rebekah was the one who would be Isaac's wife, Abraham's servant gave Rebekah and her family
   a. a homemade pizza, extra cheese
   b. silver, gold, and precious gifts
   c. whatever they asked for
   d. blessings from Abraham

5. What did Jesus use to generously feed five thousand men (plus women and children) who'd come out to hear Him teach?

    a. a food truck
    b. five loaves and two fishes
    c. the cattle on a thousand hills
    d. quail and manna

6. When the Queen of Sheba visited King Solomon, she brought him much gold and spices. In return, King Solomon gave her

    a. half his kingdom
    b. many servants
    c. lots of olive oil
    d. whatever she asked for

7. What did Dorcas make and give to the poor people of her city of Joppa?

    a. clay pots
    b. clothing
    c. medicine
    d. glazed doughnuts

❀ ANSWERS ❀

1. a (Mark 10:21)

2. c (Luke 19:8)

3. c (Acts 3:1–8)

4. b (Genesis 24:53)

5. b (Matthew 14:17–21)

6. d (1 Kings 10:13)

7. b (Acts 9:39)

⇒ QUIZ 17 ⇐
GOOD DEEDS
(doing things helpful to others)

Before Jesus left the earth to return to His Father in heaven, He told His disciple Peter, "Feed my sheep." When Jesus said "sheep," He meant people. Jesus wanted Peter to "feed" His people by reminding them that Jesus had come to save them from sin.

In England during World War II, almost two thousand years after Jesus went back to heaven, Bessie Adams remembered Jesus' words: "Feed my sheep." And that is exactly what she and her husband did. They brought God's Word, the Bible, to the people.

Bessie and Ken Adams saw that much of what the people read about Jesus and God was untrue. So they rented a small apartment where they sold Bibles and other true Christian writings.

By the end of the war, they had opened six book-stores in England. But Bessie and Ken didn't stop there. They began a mission called Christian Literature Crusade with the idea to feed God's Word to people all around the world. Today their mission, CLC, serves fifty-eight countries with more than a thousand men and women continuing to bring true Christian writings to Jesus' "sheep."

That is the best good deed you can do for anyone. But there are other good deeds God wants you to do just like these people in this quiz.

1. Dorcas helped the poor by sewing clothes for them. When she died, the people she had helped begged Peter to do something. So,
   a. he handed out Kleenex
   b. he prayed, then raised Dorcas from the dead
   c. he learned how to sew
   d. he organized a clothing drive

2. The Pharisees used trumpets to announce their good deeds so that people would admire them. Jesus said
   a. God would not reward the Pharisees for that
   b. kazoos should be used instead of trumpets
   c. they were good men
   d. you should do that too

3. Jesus told a parable about a man who did a very good deed by taking care of another man who had been robbed and beaten. That parable is called
   a. The Lost Sheep
   b. Lazarus and the Rich Man
   c. The Pearl of Great Price
   d. The Good Samaritan

4. When Naaman found out he had leprosy, his wife's maid did a good deed and told Naaman's wife that he should
   a. go see the prophet Elisha for a cure
   b. visit the king's nurse
   c. wash in the Pool of Siloam
   d. try some calamine lotion

5. When Joseph was in prison in Egypt, he helped Pharaoh's cupbearer and baker by
a. teaching them Hebrew
b. interpreting their dreams
c. telling the guards to go easy on them
d. getting them jobs in the prison kitchen

6. What does the book of James say our good deeds prove?
a. our wisdom
b. our education
c. our faith in God
d. all the above

7. Jesus said that you should let your light shine before men so they could see your good deeds and
a. do the same
b. bless you
c. honor your Father in heaven
d. not stumble in the darkness

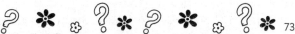

❀ ANSWERS ❀

1. b (Acts 9:39–41)

2. a (Matthew 6:2–4)

3. d (Luke 10:30–37)

4. a (2 Kings 5:1–3)

5. b (Genesis 40:8)

6. c (James 2:14)

7. c (Matthew 5:16)

➤ QUIZ 18 ⟜

GROWING UP

(becoming older and wiser)

Who was Jairus's daughter? The Bible doesn't say much about her, not even her name, only that she was twelve years old and very sick. Her dad, Jairus, worried she might die. But he believed there was still hope in Jesus. He trusted that Jesus could heal his daughter, if only he could get to Him and ask.

Wherever Jesus went, crowds followed. A sea of people stood between Jairus and Jesus. He pushed his way through. Finally, he reached Jesus and said, "My little daughter is almost dead. Will You come so she may be healed and live?" Jairus knew time was running out for his girl.

Jesus went with Jairus, and so did the crowd. Everyone wanted to see what Jesus would do. Some of Jairus's friends arrived with sad news. Time had run out. His little girl had died!

Can you imagine how Jairus felt? "Jairus," Jesus said, "do not be afraid. Only believe." Then Jesus went with Jairus into his house. He ordered the crowd to stay outside. Jesus held the dead girl's hand and told her, "Little girl, get up!" She opened her eyes, and she was well! Because of Jesus that little girl lived to grow up.

It's not easy growing up. There is so much to learn. Maybe these examples will teach you some important lessons.

1. This boy's mother, Hannah, dedicated him to the Lord—so he grew up in the temple with the priest, Eli.
   a. Samuel
   b. Samson
   c. Saul
   d. Solomon

2. How old was Jesus when His parents lost Him in Jerusalem and found Him in the temple talking with the religious teachers?
   a. 3
   b. 5
   c. 7
   d. 12

3. The Bible says that Jesus grew strong in mind and body and in favor with God and
   a. parents
   b. men
   c. cousins
   d. friends

4. Why did God tell the prophet Samuel to choose young David to be the next king instead of an older brother?
   a. "he has the biggest muscles"
   b. "this man is my chosen instrument to proclaim my name to the Gentiles"
   c. "he is without blame, a man who is right and good"
   d. "man looks at the outside of a person, but the Lord looks at the heart"

5. What Old Testament prophet questioned his calling by telling God, "I am only a boy"?
a. Jeremiah
b. Obadiah
c. Moses
d. Habakkuk

6. How did God respond to the boy-prophet of question 5?
a. "Before you were born, I set you apart as holy"
b. "Do not be afraid. . .for I am with you"
c. "I have chosen you this day"
d. all the above

7. The youngest king of Judah was seven years old when he took the throne. His name was
a. Jesus
b. Saul
c. Joash
d. Jonathan

✿ ANSWERS ✿

1. a (1 Samuel 1:20, 24–28)

2. d (Luke 2:42)

3. b (Luke 2:52)

4. d (1 Samuel 16:7–12)

5. a (Jeremiah 1:1–6)

6. d (Jeremiah 1:4–10)

7. c (2 Chronicles 22:10–23:11)

HELPING

(giving someone a hand)

Dorcas (also called Tabitha) was a follower of Jesus. Jesus' love shone through her as she did many good deeds and acts of kindness, mainly for the poor.

Dorcas sewed beautiful clothing. She could have sold her clothing to the rich, but instead she gave it to the poor. Women who had nothing and were alone caring for their families, those whose husbands had died, wore Dorcas's beautiful clothes.

One day Dorcas became sick and died. The women in Joppa cried and mourned, but then they remembered Jesus' disciple Peter was in a nearby town. They sent for him, and Peter came at once. He went to the room where Dorcas's body lay, and he sent the women away.

Peter got on his knees and prayed for a miracle. "Tabitha, get up!" he said. God answered Peter's prayer. Dorcas opened her eyes and sat up. Peter invited the women back into the room. They could hardly believe their eyes! News of this spread through Joppa, and because of it many more people put their trust in Jesus as Savior.

The important lesson in Dorcas's story isn't that she was raised from the dead, but that she served God with her many acts of kindness.

As you answer these quiz questions, maybe you will come up with a way you can help someone today.

1. Baby Moses' mother, Jochebed, sent the boy's sister to watch over him while he floated on a river in a basket. Moses' sister was named
   a. Maureen
   b. Eve
   c. Miriam
   d. Ruth

2. Which of Jesus' disciples brought his brother, Peter, to meet Jesus?
   a. Andrew
   b. James
   c. John
   d. Paul

3. When King Saul was upset, David played soothing music for him on what instrument?
   a. tambourine
   b. harp
   c. trumpet
   d. electric guitar

4. The apostle Paul said Jesus had taught that we are happiest
   a. when we give rather than receive
   b. after we have worked hard for others
   c. falling asleep while praying for people
   d. if we build churches in foreign lands

5. Who helped Daniel get back out of the lions' den?
a. his mother, who raised him
b. his father, who taught him
c. his friends, who loved him
d. the king, who put him there

6. God told Elijah to hide from wicked King Ahab. Then God helped Elijah by sending ravens to bring him
a. sticks for a fire
b. manna and bananas
c. bread and meat
d. macaroni and cheese

7. The Golden Rule says you are to help other people by doing for them
a. whatever they ask
b. what Jesus has done for you
c. what others have done for you
d. what you would like them to do for you

❁ ANSWERS ❁

1. c (Exodus 2:3-4; Numbers 26:59)

2. a (John 1:40-41)

3. b (1 Samuel 16:23)

4. a (Acts 20:35)

5. d (Daniel 6:23)

6. c (1 Kings 17:6)

7. d (Matthew 7:12)

HOPE

(believing good things will happen as God promised)

Even those who don't read the Bible know this Mary's story. It's a lesson about trusting God when you don't understand why He has led you into an unbelievable situation.

Mary was a young woman planning her wedding. She and her fiancé, Joseph, made promises to each other. One of them was that they wouldn't have a baby until after they were married.

But then her plans changed. Mary was going about her work when God's angel, Gabriel, appeared from nowhere. "Greetings!" he said. "The Lord has blessed you and is with you." Mary was very afraid.

The angel said, "Don't be afraid, Mary; God has shown you His grace. Listen! You will become pregnant and give birth to a son, and you will name him Jesus. He will be great and will be called the Son of the Most High."

Mary was excited because she knew that her Son was the promised Messiah, the Savior Israel had been hoping for. Now that hope was coming true.

Have you ever hoped for something and then got it? That feels awesome! Now let's see what else you know about hope. Maybe you'll learn some things that will help you build up even more hope.

1. What did the apostle Paul tell Titus was the Christian's "great (or blessed) hope"?
   a. healthy and wealth
   b. world peace
   c. the second coming of Jesus
   d. a happy family

2. The prophet Jeremiah said that God has plans for His people, plans to give them hope and a
   a. blessing
   b. past
   c. sign
   d. future

3. The Bible says faith is being sure of what you hope for and
   a. what you once had
   b. what you are told
   c. what you can't see
   d. what you have

4. When the children of Israel were slaves in Egypt, they hoped for someone to save them. Who did God send?
   a. Pharaoh
   b. Joshua
   c. Adam
   d. Moses

5. The apostle Paul said hope is one of three things that will last when everything else is gone. The other two things are:
   a. faith and love
   b. worry and doubt
   c. soul and spirit
   d. fire and water

6. Hannah was glad God gave her the son she had hoped for. When he was born she named him
   a. Samuel
   b. Samson
   c. Shadrach
   d. Sennacherib

7. How does the book of Hebrews describe our Christian hope?
   a. as food for the soul
   b. as oxygen for the soul
   c. as peace for the soul
   d. as an anchor for the soul

❀ ANSWERS ❀

1. c (Titus 2:13)

2. d (Jeremiah 29:11)

3. c (Hebrews 11:1)

4. d (Exodus 3:11)

5. a (1 Corinthians 13:13)

6. a (1 Samuel 1:19–20)

7. d (Hebrews 6:19)

HOSPITALITY

(friendly and kind treatment
of guests or strangers)

When company comes to your house, how do you prepare? You do everything you can think of to make your
guests feel welcome. You put your whole heart into
entertaining them by going out of your way to be warm,
generous, and kind. Making company feel welcome is
called *hospitality*, and it's a good thing.

What if your guest was Jesus?

Mary and Martha were grown-up sisters and Jesus'
close friends. They lived together, and whenever Jesus
and His disciples came to their village, Jesus stayed
with them.

Martha was all about hospitality. Imagine how con-
cerned she became when Jesus arrived in their village. She had no warning. There were no smartphones
back then. Jesus couldn't call or text to say He was
coming. He just showed up. And when He did, Martha
got busy.

When Jesus arrived, Martha was making supper.
She and Mary welcomed their friend in. Martha made
supper and made sure Jesus was comfortable.

In what ways do you make people comfortable
when they come to visit you? If you want some more
ideas of how to practice hospitality, you will be sure to
find them in the following quiz.

1. The book of Hebrews says that when you are hospitable to strangers sometimes you are actually entertaining _____ without knowing it.
   a. celebrities
   b. escaped prisoners
   c. superheroes
   d. angels

2. Jesus often stayed at the home of Lazarus and Lazarus's two sisters
   a. Ruth and Naomi
   b. Rachel and Leah
   c. Mary and Martha
   d. Jezebel and Athaliah

3. When Solomon was king, he showed hospitality by having the Queen of Sheba for a visit. Why did she come?
   a. she had heard of Solomon's fame
   b. she wanted to borrow some money
   c. she was visiting all the rulers in the Middle East
   d. she took a wrong turn on the highway

4. When a Pharisee named Simon hosted Jesus, the Lord corrected Simon because
   a. the food ran out
   b. the host was upset by a woman who washed Jesus' feet
   c. the house was dirty
   d. all the above

5. Which church leaders are supposed to be especially good at hospitality?

a. music directors
b. Sunday school teachers
c. pastors and elders
d. curriculum writers

6. When three men sent by God visited Abraham, he immediately

a. gave them a drink of water
b. told Sarah to bake bread for them
c. made them an offering
d. offered them his tent

7. To help uncover a plot against her people, Esther used hospitality and invited the king and the wicked man named _____ to a banquet.

a. Saul
b. Ahab
c. Haman
d. Judas

❀ ANSWERS ❀

1. d (Hebrews 13:2)

2. c (John 11:1-3)

3. a (2 Chronicles 9:1)

4. b (Luke 7:36-50)

5. c (Titus 1:5-9)

6. b (Genesis 18:1-7)

7. c (Esther 5:4)

INFLUENCE
(using power to convince someone for good)

Paul was like a father to Timothy. He shared wise advice with this younger Christian friend, and in his letter Paul also wrote about Timothy's faith. He said, "I remember your true faith. It is the same faith your grandmother Lois had and your mother Eunice had" (2 Timothy 1:5).

From Paul's words, we know that Lois was Timothy's grandmother and that she had "true faith." She taught Timothy to have that kind of faith too. That's all the Bible tells us about Lois. She was probably like many grandmothers today who love their children, grandchildren—and Jesus!

A Lois kind of grandma is an older woman who believes without doubting that Jesus is the only way to heaven. She trusts Jesus as Savior and loves Him because He loves us. And when her faith is tested, a Lois kind of grandma stays strong. Nothing can stop her from trusting God! She wants her children and grandchildren to have true faith too. So she teaches them about Jesus and leads them to trust Him.

Lois grandmothers are a good influence in the lives of kids. As you take the quiz, take note of which influencers are good and which are bad—and stick with only the good in your own life!

1. Influence can be good or bad. Only one queen of Israel and one queen of Judah are mentioned by name in the Bible and they happen to be wicked and mother and daughter. Their names are
   a. Jezebel and Athaliah
   b. Ruth and Naomi
   c. Mary and Martha
   d. Leah and Dinah

2. Paul told Timothy that Timothy's faith was strong because of Lois and Eunice who were Timothy's
   a. two older sisters
   b. grandmother and mother
   c. church deacons
   d. Sunday school teachers

3. Jesus was a very good influence on people because He went about doing good and teaching people about the kingdom of God. Jesus did what He did because
   a. He was doing what His Father God taught Him
   b. He was doing what Moses told Him to do
   c. He wanted fame and fortune
   d. He wanted the disciples to like Him

4. Paul called Titus "my true son in the faith" because
   a. Titus was Paul's son
   b. it was Paul who taught Titus to believe in Jesus
   c. Titus was Jewish, like Jesus
   d. Titus had married Paul's daughter

5. The Lord said Ahaziah was a wicked king because Ahaziah chose to walk in the wicked ways of his grandfather

    a. King Ahab

    b. King Absalom

    c. King Saul

    d. King Hezekiah

6. When Peter preached his first sermon on the day of Pentecost and told all the people how Jesus had come just like the scriptures said He would

    a. the people called Peter a liar

    b. the apostles applauded

    c. about 3,000 people were saved and baptized

    d. the high priest threw Peter into jail

7. What did John the Baptist call Jesus, causing two of his disciples to follow the Lord?

    a. the Creator of Heaven and Earth

    b. the Voice of One in the Wilderness

    c. the Power from On High

    d. the Lamb of God

❀ ANSWERS ❀

1. a (1 Kings 19:1–2; 2 Kings 9:30; 11:1)

2. b (2 Timothy 1:5)

3. a (John 8:28)

4. b (Titus 1:4)

5. a (2 Kings 8:27)

6. c (Acts 2:41)

7. d (John 1:35–37)

JOY

(a feeling of great happiness or delight)

There are six Marys in the Bible. They include Mary, Jesus' mother; Mary, sister of Martha, from the village of Bethany; and Mary Magdalene from a place called Magdala near the Sea of Galilee.

If you had known Mary Magdalene, you might have called her "Grateful Mary." The Bible says she was possessed by seven demons that made her sick, and Jesus cast them out (Mark 16:9; Luke 8:2). Jesus made her better, and she was grateful. We know Mary loved Jesus, because she became one of His followers.

Her story continues on the day Jesus died on the cross. Mary was there. How sad she must have felt seeing Him suffering. How terrible when He died. Friends put Jesus' body into a tomb and sealed it with a rock.

Three days later, Mary went to the tomb and found the rock moved away. Jesus' body was gone. "Where have they put Him?" she asked, crying. Then Mary turned and saw Jesus standing there alive. "Teacher!" Oh, how grateful she was to see Him. He had come back, just as He promised His followers He would.

Jesus told Mary Magdalene to spread the Good News, and she became known as the first person ever to tell others, "He lives!"

Let's see what more the Bible teaches about joy as you answer these quiz questions.

1. Psalm 100 says "Call out with joy to the Lord, all
_____."
a. the earth
b. you people
c. you shepherds
d. of nature

2. What does the book of Nehemiah say "the joy of
the Lord" is?
a. your health
b. your reward
c. your strength
d. your blessing

3. Jesus said that there is more joy in heaven over one
sinner who is sorry for his sins than over ninety-nine
people who
a. are right with God
b. are happy in their sins
c. go to church every Sunday
d. have never heard of Jesus

4. How old was John the Baptist when he first felt joy
by learning about his relative, Jesus the Son of God?
a. 2 years
b. 6 years
c. 20 years
d. he was still in his mother's belly

5. God loves you so much that He has much joy in you and rejoices over you with
   a. gladness
   b. singing
   c. love
   d. angels

6. The Bible says that weeping and sadness may remain for a night but joy
   a. never comes on time
   b. comes with the new day
   c. remains for two nights
   d. has a way of finding you

7. What event caused David to dance with joy before the Lord?
   a. his victory over Goliath
   b. the birth of his son Solomon
   c. his marriage to Saul's daughter Michal
   d. the arrival of the ark of the covenant in his capital city

❁ ANSWERS ❁

1. a (Psalm 100:1)

2. c (Nehemiah 8:10)

3. a (Luke 15:7)

4. d (Luke 1:41)

5. b (Zephaniah 3:17)

6. b (Psalm 30:5)

7. c (2 Samuel 6:16)

⇾ QUIZ 24 ⇽
KEEPING PROMISES
(doing what you say you'll do)

When the Israelites arrived at the land God promised them, they found the Canaanites living there.

The Israelites' leader, Joshua, sent two spies into the city of Jericho. There was a woman living there who was well known in the city, but not in a good way. Rahab didn't live a godly life, but God wanted her to help His people. She hid the spies in her house.

Someone saw the spies enter Rahab's house and told Jericho's king. It wasn't unusual for Rahab to have men over, so the king thought maybe she didn't know they were spies. He sent a message telling her who the men were and ordering her to bring them out. Rahab lied, saying, "They've already gone."

When it was safe for the spies to leave, Rahab reminded them she had saved their lives. She said, "I have shown you kindness. . . . Promise me by the Lord that you will show kindness to those of my father's house" (Joshua 2:12). She asked the spies to promise that she and her family would be safe when the Israelites came and took the land.

The spies promised, and they kept their promise. When the Israelites destroyed everything in the city, they rescued Rahab and her family because Rahab had helped them.

Let's see what more you can learn about keeping promises as you take this quiz.

1. What did the Israelite spies tell Rahab to put in her window so the army could recognize her house and keep their promise to her?
    a. a red rope
    b. a potted plant
    c. a water jug
    d. a bird cage

2. God promised Noah that God would never again flood the earth. The sign that God would keep that promise was
    a. a rainbow in the sky
    b. a cloud shaped like an umbrella
    c. a dove with an olive leaf in her beak
    d. the man in the moon

3. God promised Abraham that God would give him a son. How old was Abraham when his son Isaac was born?
    a. 20
    b. 30
    c. 50
    d. 100

4. God promised the people of Israel that a Messiah would come and deliver them from all their sins. That Messiah was
    a. John the Baptist
    b. Elijah
    c. Jesus
    d. Moses

5. When you make a promise to God, the Bible says you should fulfill it right away. Because God is not pleased with
   a. fools
   b. promise breakers
   c. daydreamers
   d. sinners

6. After Jesus rose from the dead and right before He ascended into heaven, "men dressed in white" promised His disciples that
   a. Jesus would rain down pennies from heaven
   b. they would speak before kings
   c. Jesus would come back the same way He left
   d. they would one day wear white

7. God promised Moses that on the night all the first-born of the Egyptians would die, the Israelites would be saved if they put blood on their doorposts. What was this event later called?
   a. Passover
   b. Pentecost
   c. Easter
   d. Epiphany

✿ ANSWERS ✿

1. a (Joshua 2:17–18)

2. a (Genesis 9:12–13)

3. d (Genesis 17:17)

4. c (Matthew 1:21)

5. a (Ecclesiastes 5:4–5)

6. c (Acts 1:11)

7. a (Exodus 12:12–13. Because God "passed over" the homes with the blood!)

KINDNESS

(being good or nice to someone)

The Bible says Lydia sold purple cloth. That doesn't tell us much about her, but when we think of Lydia living back in the first century, we can guess at a few other things. She owned a business, which was unusual for women of her time. And she probably had money— because purple was the color worn by royalty, and the rich bought her cloth.

Lydia lived in Philippi. Some people there believed in the one true God, but they hadn't heard about Jesus. Lydia was one of them. One day she went with some women to a peaceful area near a river to pray. There she met Timothy and Paul. She listened as Paul talked about Jesus being the only way to heaven. Lydia believed his words and invited Jesus into her heart.

Lydia became the first person in Europe to become a Christian! But her story doesn't end there. She invited Paul and Timothy to stay at her house. Then Lydia told others and helped to spread the Good News. While Paul was in Philippi, he and his friends were always welcome in her home.

Lydia showed kindness to Paul and Timothy by giving them a place to stay and helping them spread the Good News. How kind do you think God wants you to be? Maybe you can answer that question by taking this quiz.

1. When did the leader of the island of Malta show kindness to Paul and his missionary team, by giving them everything they needed?
   a. after Paul had been beaten with rods
   b. after Paul had been stoned
   c. after Paul was released from jail
   d. after Paul was shipwrecked

2. Years after Joseph's brothers sold him into slavery, he showed kindness to them by
   a. giving them food
   b. giving them a meal at his house
   c. forgiving them for selling him into slavery
   d. all the above

3. Jesus once showed kindness to a widow who lived in a town called Nain. What did he do for her?
   a. find her a husband
   b. give her money
   c. raise her son from the dead
   d. buy her a puppy

4. In Jesus' story about being a good neighbor, the Good Samaritan showed kindness by
   a. taking care of the animals in his village
   b. helping a total stranger who had been beaten and robbed
   c. cleaning his neighbor's house
   d. washing his mayor's chariot

5. When the children of Israel wandered in the wilderness for 40 years, God showed them kindness by giving them *manna*. That name means

    a. what is it?
    b. God's gift
    c. white food
    d. is this rice?

6. Obadiah was in charge of wicked King Ahab's palace. When King Ahab's wicked wife, Jezebel, tried to kill all the prophets of God, Obadiah showed kindness to 100 of those prophets by

    a. giving them airline fare to fly home
    b. helping them find shields
    c. hiding them in caves and feeding them
    d. helping them secretly leave Israel

7. After Jonathan died, his best friend David wanted to show kindness to Jonathan's family. David took Mephibosheth into his own family. Mephibosheth was Jonathan's

    a. father
    b. brother
    c. cousin
    d. son

❀ ANSWERS ❀

1. d (Acts 27:40–28:7)

2. d (Genesis 43:26–44:2; 45:4–8)

3. c (Luke 7:11–15)

4. b (Luke 10:33–35)

5. a (Exodus 16:15)

6. c (1 Kings 18:13)

7. d (2 Samuel 9:1–7)

LEADERSHIP

(being in charge; showing by example how to do good things)

When Margaret Baxter lived—in Puritan times—men made the rules. Women were expected to follow them, live quietly, and be happy at home doing household chores. But that wasn't Margaret's style! In her mind, she and her husband were a team, and that caused others to think of her as a "public-spirited woman"—in those days, not a good thing.

Margaret's husband, Henry, was a well-known English preacher and church leader, but he wasn't the quickest at problem solving. On the other hand, Margaret could decide right away what was wrong, and she wasn't afraid to tell Henry how to fix it.

It was unusual for a man to take a woman's advice back then, but Henry recognized Margaret's gift for getting to the root of a problem. He said, "Her reasons usually told me that she was in the right." Henry also defended his wife when others accused her of being too busy with church and charities. He reminded them that the apostle Paul had welcomed women to help spread God's Word. Margaret was a wise leader. You can be a leader too, and nothing can stop you. Look around! Female leaders are everywhere

The people in this quiz were leaders. What can you learn about how to be a leader from them?

1. Moses sent 12 spies into Canaan to see if the Israelites could successfully take over their Promised Land. The two spies who said, "Yes, we can," were named
   a. Bert and Ernie
   b. Jonathan and David
   c. Abraham and Isaac
   d. Joshua and Caleb

2. After Saul became a follower of Christ, the other disciples were still afraid of him. Who showed leadership by welcoming the man who once tried to hurt the church?
   a. Barnabas
   b. Tertius
   c. Onesimus
   d. Agabus

3. When God told Solomon to ask for anything he wanted, Solomon asked for _____ so he could be a good king and leader of his people.
   a. a queen
   b. a throne
   c. a palace
   d. understanding

4. When John was in exile on the Island of Patmos, he saw visions of things to come. One of those visions was about the armies of heaven. And the leader of those armies was
   a. John himself
   b. Jesus the King of kings
   c. Michael the archangel
   d. the apostle Peter

5. Nicodemus, who came to see Jesus secretly at night, was a member of the Jewish ruling council called the Sanhedrin. Nicodemus was also
   a. a leper
   b. blind
   c. a Pharisee
   d. a spy

6. When Paul encouraged Timothy as a church leader, what did the apostle say people should not disrespect about Timothy?
   a. that he was short
   b. that he was poor
   c. that he was sickly
   d. that he was young

7. The only woman who was a judge (or leader) of Israel was
   a. Mary
   b. Deborah
   c. Eve
   d. Martha

❀ ANSWERS ❀

1. d (Numbers 13:16, 30)

2. a (Acts 9:26–30)

3. d (1 Kings 3:7–9)

4. b (Revelation 19:11–16)

5. c (John 3:1–2)

6. d (1 Timothy 4:12)

7. b (Judges 4:4)

~ QUIZ 27 ~
LEARNING
(getting to know someone or something)

Mary McLeod Bethune was born not long after the Civil War. She watched her family and other former slaves struggle to make a life free from slavery. Mary's mom continued to work for her former owner until she earned enough money to buy the land where the family grew cotton. Maybe it was her mother's strong example combined with faith in God that made Mary work extra hard.

African-American children were finally free to attend school. When a missionary opened a school in her area, Mary walked miles to go there and learn. And learn she did! She grew up to graduate from college and become a teacher. But that wasn't enough. She wanted to provide the best education for all African-American children, so she rented a tiny cottage and opened a school. At first she had six students. Then more came. And more. Mary's school grew and grew. Mary knew that learning and knowledge were the keys to helping people become independent.

Mary's love of learning and her hard work got the attention of President Franklin D. Roosevelt. He chose her as his adviser to help bring all Americans together as equals, whatever the color of their skin.

Learning can be fun and lead you places—perhaps some places where God wants you to go. Now let's see what you can learn from the quiz.

1. Which of the following is *not* a time Moses told the Israelites to teach God's Word to their kids?

a. when you sit
b. when you go swimming
c. when you lie down
d. when you walk on the road

2. Priscilla and her husband Aquila taught this person more things about God:

a. Amos
b. Adam
c. Apollos
d. Absalom

3. What powerful country sent the young Jewish men Daniel, Shadrach, Meshach, and Abednego to school in order to serve its king?

a. Assyria
b. Greece
c. Babylon
d. Russia

4. Samuel's mother dedicated Samuel to the Lord. Then she brought Samuel to the Temple so he could learn

a. to serve and worship the Lord
b. to be the next king
c. to tend the priests' sheep
d. to play the harp

5. According to the book of Proverbs, what kind of person grows in learning?

   a. wise
   b. wealthy
   c. winsome
   d. wonderful

6. When Jesus was 12, Mary and Joseph found Him in the Temple sitting among the teachers listening to them and asking them questions. The Bible says that Jesus grew

   a. in mind
   b. in body
   c. in favor with God and men
   d. all the above

7. Martha's sister Mary learned from Jesus because she sat at His feet and

   a. listened to Him speak
   b. read her Bible
   c. asked Him questions
   d. tuned in a podcast

✿ ANSWERS ✿

1. b (Deuteronomy 6:7. But you could learn
   God's Word even then!)

2. c (Acts 18:24–26)

3. c (Daniel 1:1–7)

4. a (1 Samuel 1:28)

5. a (Proverbs 1:5)

6. d (Luke 2:52)

7. a (Luke 10:39)

LOVE
(selfless concern for others)

Jane Austen is one of the most famous nineteenth-century English authors. She was a Christian who hid valuable life lessons in her work. Jane's stories don't usually mention God like the Bible and some other books do; instead, they show how God wants us to live.

If you read Jane's stories, you will discover that her main characters learn good lessons about godly values like honesty, humility—not thinking that you are better than others—and overcoming prejudice. Her characters learn to understand each other better and accept one another just as they are.

Maybe because Jane recognized that God's love is everywhere, she often hid messages about love in her stories.

Growing up the daughter of a minister, Jane knew and loved God. She and her family shared God's love by helping others. While she might not have written boldly about her faith, Jane's faith was strong. When she died, she received the honor of being buried at a famous church (Winchester Cathedral), not because she was an important author, but because she was well known for serving God.

You show your love for God by serving Him. What can you learn about love from this quiz?

1. According to the book of Romans, how did God prove His love for the world?
   a. by creating the sunshine
   b. by providing the Bible
   c. by putting a rainbow in the sky
   d. by sending Jesus to die for sinners

2. God the Father's love is so great through Jesus that we should be called
   a. God's children
   b. Christians
   c. churchgoers
   d. God's creation

3. Jacob loved and wanted to marry Rachel. But Rachel's father, Laban, tricked Jacob into marrying her sister
   a. Ruth
   b. Mary
   c. Leah
   d. Esther

4. Jesus said that the first and greatest instruction in the law was
   a. love the Lord your God with all your heart, soul, and mind
   b. be kind and loving to strangers who may be angels
   c. love and obey your parents and things will go well
   d. eat your brussels sprouts

5. The book of Proverbs says that hate starts fights, but that love covers all
a. people
b. sins
c. enemies
d. friends

6. According to Jesus, what would Christians' love for each other prove to everyone else?
a. that they are His followers
b. that they should be respected
c. that they know what is right
d. that they will change the world

7. According to the book of 1 John, what is something that Christians are *not* supposed to love?
a. scary movies
b. bad language
c. expensive clothing
d. the world or anything in it

  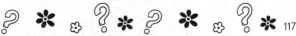

❀ ANSWERS ❀

1. d (Romans 5:8)

2. a (1 John 3:1)

3. c (Genesis 29:16–25. That's not a good
   situation.)

4. a (Matthew 22:37–38)

5. b (Proverbs 10:12)

6. a (John 13:34–35)

7. d (1 John 2:15)

MEEKNESS

(being quiet and self-controlled)

Ruth grew up in Moab. Her husband Mahlon was from Bethlehem, a town about fifty miles away. He had moved to Moab with his parents when he was a boy. Life hadn't been easy for Mahlon. Before he came to Moab, his family had suffered through a famine—they had little food to eat. Then, after they moved, his father died. Then Mahlon died too!

Ruth and her mother-in-law had only each other.

Naomi heard things had gotten better in Bethlehem. So Ruth and her mother-in-law packed their things and started walking. Ruth was willing to leave the place where she had lived all her life so Naomi wouldn't be alone.

On the way, Naomi understood how much Ruth was giving up to be with her. She said, "Go back home! God bless you for being so kind to me."

But Ruth refused to leave Naomi. She said, "Do not beg me to leave you or turn away from following you. I will go where you go. I will live where you live. Your people will be my people. And your God will be my God" (Ruth 1:16–17).

Ruth showed her meekness by being willing to do whatever Naomi said. In the quiz that follows, you can learn much more about God and how much He admires meekness in His people.

1. What did the apostle Peter say a woman's meekness—her gentle and quiet spirit—is?

a. treasure
b. beauty
c. a gift to the world
d. victory over Satan

2. Job showed meekness through all his sufferings by saying he would trust God even if God _____ him.

a. forgot
b. killed
c. crushed
d. fought

3. Moses is an excellent example of meekness because of the way he dealt with the grumbling of the children of Israel as they wandered in the wilderness for _____ years.

a. 10
b. 20
c. 30
d. 40

4. Jesus is the greatest example of meekness. Even though the soldiers nailed Him to the cross, Jesus said, "Father, forgive them for they. . .

a. do not know what they are doing"
b. don't really mean to kill Me"
c. have no idea who I am"
d. are ignorant Romans"

5. In the Sermon on the Mount, Jesus said people who are meek or have no pride are
a. hopeful
b. happy
c. human
d. hearty

6. In the book of Galatians (KJV), the apostle Paul says that meekness is a
a. good thing
b. bad thing
c. fruit of the Spirit
d. a lesson to be learned

7. Jesus says you should follow His teachings and learn from Him. Because He is meek, what will you find with Him?
a. joy in your home
b. hope for your future
c. wisdom for your exams
d. rest for your soul

❁ ANSWERS ❁

1. b (1 Peter 3:4)

2. b (Job 13:15)

3. d (Numbers 32:13)

4. a (Luke 23:34)

5. b (Matthew 5:5. Some Bible translations say "blessed.")

6. c (Galatians 5:22–23)

7. d (Matthew 11:29)

❧ QUIZ 30 ❧
MERCY

(kindness by one who has power over another)

Mary Slessor was a Scottish missionary in Africa. She dared to go deep into the areas where native African tribes lived. Few missionaries had the courage to go there, especially women. They feared they wouldn't survive.

Superstition existed everywhere among the tribes, and they were preoccupied with demons, spirits, and false gods. One of their worst beliefs was that if a woman gave birth to twins, the second-born was controlled by an evil spirit. If a mom had twins, the tribes abandoned her and the babies and left them in the jungle to die.

Mary believed only in the one true God, and her mission was to show mercy to those who were treated badly because of false beliefs. Mary opened up a house for the twins who were left behind. Some of the moms came too. Mary cared for them and treated the children as if they were her own.

Mary taught the people about Jesus, and even when they were not accepting of Him, she was merciful—kind and caring—toward them.

God is merciful toward you, forgiving you for your faults and loving you anyway. How can you show mercy to others? If you're not sure, perhaps you will get some ideas as you look at the quiz that follows.

1. While Samson was a slave in prison, God showed mercy to him by letting his hair grow back and giving Samson back
   a. his dignity
   b. his strength
   c. his sight
   d. his pride

2. In the parable of the Pharisee and the tax collector, the Pharisee bragged about himself but the tax collector asked God to have pity or mercy on him because he was
   a. a sinner
   b. a good man
   c. a father of ten
   d. a friend of Jesus

3. God said He would show mercy to how many generations of the people that love Him and keep His commandments?
   a. 13
   b. 52
   c. hundreds
   d. thousands

4. In the Sermon on the Mount, Jesus said, "Blessed are the merciful (KJV)" because they will be shown
   a. love
   b. peace
   c. mercy
   d. off

5. Jesus showed mercy to a man that was possessed by many evil spirits. Jesus made the evil spirits leave the man and go into a nearby

    a. flock of doves
    b. flock of sheep
    c. herd of pigs
    d. herd of cows

6. As Jesus and His disciples were leaving Jericho one day, two blind beggars begged Jesus to have mercy on them. Jesus stopped and

    a. gave them money
    b. gave them new clothes
    c. gave them their sight
    d. all the above

7. God says He will have mercy on whom?

    a. anyone He wants to
    b. those who really need it
    c. anyone who gives money to church
    d. those who get to Him first

❀ ANSWERS ❀

1. b (Judges 16:21–30)

2. a (Luke 18:13)

3. d (Exodus 20:6)

4. c (Matthew 5:7)

5. c (Mark 5:1–13)

6. c (Matthew 20:29–34)

7. a (Romans 9:15–16)

NEARNESS TO GOD

(really knowing God personally)

When Jeanette Li was a little girl in South China, her father, a Buddhist, worshipped idols instead of the one true God. Something in Jeanette's heart told her this was wrong. Her mother felt it too. Neither knew then about the real God and Jesus.

Jeanette heard about Jesus when she was seven. Sick with a fever, she was at a missionary hospital. There, doctors told her God sent Jesus to die on the cross so everyone could be forgiven for their sins and live in heaven with Him forever. Jeanette prayed and asked Jesus into her heart. After that she attended a Christian school and was baptized at age ten. Her mother became a believer and was baptized too. Their new life in Christ was wonderful. But their family turned away from them because they had turned from the Buddhist religion. It hurt, but they believed that nothing, not even their family, could pull them away from God.

Jeanette wanted to become a teacher, and her deep, busy studying took her away from praying and reading the Bible. Thankfully, she noticed and concentrated on staying near Him. And God used Jeanette for the rest of her life.

If you ever find yourself drifting from God, run back to Him. See how much closer you can get to Him as you take the quiz that follows.

1. Hagar ran away when Sarah was being mean to her. When Hagar was all alone in the wilderness, the Lord came to her and blessed her. Hagar called the Lord "the God who. . ."

    a. sees

    b. remembers

    c. surrounds

    d. loves

2. God gave Jacob a dream of a ladder that reached from earth to heaven. On the ladder, going up and down, were

    a. sheep

    b. people

    c. angels

    d. firefighters

3. When God told Abraham He was going to destroy Sodom and Gomorrah, Abraham felt close enough to God to ask Him to spare the city if God could find at least _____ righteous people there.

    a. a thousand

    b. 300

    c. 64

    d. 10

4. When Jesus appeared in His glory to John on the Island of Patmos, John immediately fell down at Jesus' feet as if he were

    a. overjoyed

    b. dead

    c. struck blind

    d. fainting

5. When Jesus appeared to Mary Magdalene after His resurrection, she didn't recognize Him at first. She thought He was
- a. an angel
- b. the undertaker
- c. the gardener
- d. a tourist

6. Enoch is an Old Testament character who was so close to God that he
- a. was taken straight to heaven
- b. wrote the book of Judges
- c. turned water into wine
- d. parted the Jordan River

7. Anna was so close to God that she knew Jesus, the Messiah, would come in her lifetime. To be sure she didn't miss seeing Him, Anna spent every day fasting and praying
- a. at home
- b. at the city gate
- c. in the temple
- d. at Mary and Martha's house

❀ ANSWERS ❀

1. a (Genesis 16:13)

2. c (Genesis 28:12)

3. d (Genesis 18:32. The cities were destroyed and the only people who escaped were Lot, his wife, and his two daughters.)

4. b (Revelation 1:17)

5. c (John 20:15)

6. a (Genesis 5:24)

7. c (Luke 2:36–38)

OBEDIENCE

(doing as you're told)

Ann Judson was a teenager when she accepted Jesus into her heart. She studied the Bible and talked with God in prayer. She wanted God to use her. Ann asked Him to lead her where He wanted her to go.

God heard. He already had a plan for her to be a missionary on the other side of the world. Ann wouldn't be one of *many* American women missionaries overseas—she would be the first!

A young minister named Adoniram Judson was key to God's plan. He wanted to be a missionary overseas too. When he met Ann, Adoniram quickly learned that they shared that dream of faraway places. The two fell in love, got married, and sailed to India.

Burma became their home. The Burmese people accepted that Ann and Adoniram loved Jesus, but they didn't want the Lord. Ann found it hard to find words in their language to explain that Jesus came so they might live forever in heaven. Still, she tried. Ann translated the Gospel into their language. Slowly, the people began accepting Jesus.

Ann wrote about her work in Burma. After reading Ann's stories, many more American women decided to become missionaries in faraway lands. That was the best part of God's plan.

To be part of God's plan, you need to learn about obedience. You can start by taking today's quiz.

1. Peter and the other apostles told the members of the Sanhedrin, "We must obey God instead of. . ."

a. you
b. men
c. Satan
d. idols

2. What did Jesus say was true when we obey His teaching?

a. we are His followers for sure
b. we love Him
c. we live in His love
d. all the above

3. The book of Hebrews says even Jesus learned to obey by what?

a. His mother's teaching
b. time spent in the temple
c. suffering
d. reading good books

4. The apostle Paul said he worked hard to make his _____ obey him.

a. dog
b. church
c. fellow missionaries
d. body

5. What were the disciples surprised to see obeying Jesus?

a. animals and birds
b. wind and waves
c. sun and moon
d. clouds and lightning

6. Who did Esther obey when he told her she needed to talk to the king and save her people?

a. Bigthan
b. Hathach
c. Mordecai
d. the angel Gabriel

7. Samuel told King Saul, "To obey is better than _____."

a. love
b. wisdom
c. riches
d. sacrifice

❀ ANSWERS ❀

1. b (Acts 5:29)

2. d (John 8:31; John 14:21; John 15:10)

3. c (Hebrews 5:8)

4. d (1 Corinthians 9:27)

5. b (Matthew 8:27)

6. c (Esther 4:13–14)

7. d (1 Samuel 15:22 KJV)

≽ QUIZ 33 ≼
PEACEMAKING
(keeping others calm and quiet)

Corrie ten Boom grew up in the Netherlands. Her Christian family welcomed friends, neighbors, and even strangers into their home. Corrie's dad held prayer meetings at their house. He often prayed for the Jewish people, God's chosen people.

During World War II, Nazi soldiers arrested Jews for no other reason than that they were Jewish. The Nazis put them in prison camps where they suffered terribly and died.

The ten Boom family wanted to help the Jews. So Corrie and her family became part of the "Dutch underground." Corrie and her sister Betsie helped Jews escape from the Nazis by hiding them in their home. If the Nazis ever came to the house, the ten Booms hid their Jewish "guests" in a secret place behind a closet, just big enough for six.

One day someone told the Nazis what the ten Booms were doing. The Nazis arrested the ten Boom family, but the Jews hiding in the closet were not found and later escaped.

After the war, Corrie traveled the world speaking about her experience with the Nazis. She wrote about it in a bestselling book called *The Hiding Place*. Today almost everyone knows her name and story.

Corrie was a peacemaker, doing what she could to help those in need. Perhaps this quiz will help you find a way to be a peacemaker too!

1. In the Sermon on the Mount, Jesus said peacemakers are blessed and will be called
   a. a blessing
   b. happy
   c. children of God
   d. awesome

2. Abraham and his nephew, Lot, both had so many flocks and herds that their herdsmen fought each other trying to get the best land for their master's animals. To make peace, Abraham and Lot
   a. moved away from each other
   b. sold their animals
   c. hired new herdsmen
   d. offered their animals to God

3. The book of Romans says that you should live in peace with everyone. . .
   a. whenever they're nice to you
   b. as much as you can
   c. to earn your way to heaven
   d. even if they're real jerks

4. The book of James says that God's wisdom from _____ is first pure, then gives peace.
   a. Moses
   b. Paul
   c. the temple
   d. heaven

5. To keep David from killing her foolish husband, Nabal's wife, Abigail, made peace by
   a. telling David to blame her instead
   b. bringing David and his men food and drink
   c. asking David to forgive her
   d. all the above

6. What does the Bible's longest chapter—Psalm 119— say gives great peace?
   a. ten hours of sleep a night
   b. loving God's law
   c. serving as a foreign missionary
   d. playing hymns on a harp

7. How does the book of Philippians describe God's peace?
   a. "as high as the heavens"
   b. "stronger than a lion"
   c. "greater than the human mind can understand"
   d. all the above

❀ ANSWERS ❀

1. c (Matthew 5:9 KJV)

2. a (Genesis 13:9)

3. b (Romans 12:18. By the way, answer C is *totally* wrong—nobody can earn their way to heaven. That's why we need Jesus!)

4. d (James 3:17)

5. d (1 Samuel 25:18–28)

6. b (Psalm 119:165)

7. c (Philippians 4:7)

PRAYER

(asking God to use His power)

Evie Brand and her husband Jesse were missionaries serving poor people in a place called "the mountains of death."

The people there were sick. Malaria—a deadly disease carried by mosquitoes—killed many. For more than twenty-five years, Evie and Jesse did their best to help the mountain people get well. They also shared God's Word with them and started a church. But then something awful happened. Jesse got malaria and died. Evie was heartbroken! The love of her life was gone. Their two children, Connie and Paul, were in school in England. She was alone.

Evie could have given up and returned to London, but she didn't. Instead, she asked God to help her do even more. "God, give me another mountain," she prayed.

For the rest of her life, Evie stayed in India helping the mountain people. Always, she relied on God to keep her mentally and physically strong.

Evie died at age ninety-five, still working for God.

When things get hard, remember Evie. Pray that God will keep you strong every day of your life. Here are some things about prayer and examples of how other people pray.

1. When the Assyrian army surrounded Jerusalem, King Hezekiah and the prophet Isaiah prayed that God would deliver them. That night God answered their prayer by

    a. blinding the Assyrian soldiers

    b. sending His angel to kill 185,000 Assyrian soldiers

    c. causing the earth to open up and swallow the army

    d. making killer bees chase the Assyrians away

2. What did the Jews under Queen Esther add to their prayers for her safety?

    a. skipping meals for three days and nights

    b. singing psalms

    c. giving a special offering

    d. dancing a waltz

3. When Jesus was in the Garden of Gethsemane right before He was arrested, He prayed so hard that

    a. He got a headache

    b. God took Him up to heaven

    c. an army of angels landed in the garden

    d. He sweat drops like blood

4. On Mount Carmel, Elijah showed the prophets of Baal that God is the only God. Elijah prayed and

    a. God sent fire from heaven

    b. the skin of the prophets turned purple

    c. the prophets of Baal dropped dead

    d. worms ate King Ahab

5. The prophet Elijah once prayed for rain. How many times did he send his servant to look toward the sea and see if the rain was starting to fall?

    a. 2
    b. 4
    c. 6
    d. 7

6. In the Sermon on the Mount, how did Jesus describe prayer?

    a. "ask and it will be given to you"
    b. "seek and you will find"
    c. "knock and the door will be opened to you"
    d. all the above

7. The book of 1 Thessalonians says you are to pray

    a. every night before bed
    b. only on Sundays
    c. without stopping
    d. only in church

❀ ANSWERS ❀

1. b (2 Kings 19:35)

2. a (Esther 4:15–16)

3. d (Luke 22:44)

4. a (1 Kings 18:38)

5. d (1 Kings 18:41–44)

6. d (Matthew 7:7 KJV)

7. c (1 Thessalonians 5:17)

QUIETNESS

(being calm and at peace)

Teresa of Avila lived the first forty years of her life having lukewarm faith. At age twenty-one, she had entered a convent—a religious training house for women. Some convents were very strict, but at Teresa's the nuns were allowed to have their own belongings, and they could mingle with people outside. Not focusing entirely on God, Teresa believed, had caused her faith to weaken.

One day while walking in the convent, Teresa noticed a statue of Jesus on the cross. She saw it in a way she hadn't before, and she felt Christ's powerful love for her. From that day forward, Teresa's faith grew. It became so strong that she gave up everything else that mattered. She put worldly things in the past and gave all her attention to the Lord.

Quiet prayer was important to Teresa. She had the gift of understanding the spiritual life. She wrote down her ideas about prayer and living for God. Even today, more than four hundred years later, her spiritual writings are read and studied.

Teresa believed that quietness was important because it helped her focus on her prayers. What do you know about quietness? Let's find out.

1. What did the apostle Peter say a quiet spirit does for a woman?
   a. it makes her strong
   b. it makes her rich
   c. it makes her happy
   d. it makes her beautiful

2. The Proverbs say a piece of dry bread with quietness is better than a great feast with
   a. fighting
   b. loud music
   c. too much talk
   d. police sirens

3. In the book of Psalms, God tells us to be still and quiet and know
   a. He is strong
   b. He is God
   c. He is good
   d. He is mighty

4. God told the people of Israel, "Your strength will come by being quiet and. . ."
   a. trusting God
   b. singing in the choir
   c. imitating Moses
   d. lifting weights

5. Who did God speak to in a "still small voice"?

    a. Paul

    b. Moses

    c. David

    d. Elijah

6. Paul told the people in Thessalonica to learn how to be quiet, to mind their own business, and to work with. . . .

    a. mom and dad

    b. their classmates

    c. their own hands

    d. people they like

7. The Shepherd in Psalm 23 leads His sheep (who are a symbol of His followers) beside "quiet waters" to

    a. keep them safe from wolves

    b. restore their strength

    c. keep them from falling off a cliff

    d. feed them

❀ ANSWERS ❀

1. d (1 Peter 3:4)

2. a (Proverbs 17:1)

3. b (Psalm 46:10 KJV)

4. a (Isaiah 30:15)

5. d (1 Kings 19:9–13 KJV)

6. c (1 Thessalonians 4:11 KJV)

7. b (Psalm 23:2–3)

⇒ QUIZ 36 ⇐

RESISTING TEMPTATION

(choosing what God wants you to
do over what you want to do)

When God created Adam, He gave humans the gift of freedom. We are allowed so many choices, even whether to love God or not. Sometimes the most difficult choice is when we have to choose between two things so wonderful that words can't describe them. That was the kind of choice Lilias Trotter had to make.

Lilias was born with the gift of creating art. Her talent was so great she might have become one of England's best artists of the nineteenth century. But Lilias also had a heart dedicated to God. She felt Him calling her to serve as a missionary in North Africa. Lilias was tempted to choose being that or a famous artist; she chose to serve God.

Over the next forty years, Lilias traveled, often by camel, setting up mission stations—places where missionaries lived and worked. Wherever she went, Lilias carried the Word of God to the people, and many came to know Him.

She didn't give up art completely. Lilias kept journals of her travels, and she filled the pages with her beautiful work. She had given up fame to serve God, but Lilias felt content. Once she painted cottony, white seeds drifting away from a dried dandelion head. For Lilias this represented emptying herself, giving herself fully to God.

While taking this quiz, think about how you might resist temptation.

1. When Potiphar's wife tried to tempt Joseph, he
   a. kindly said no
   b. ran away
   c. screamed
   d. called the police

2. When Satan tempted Jesus, He resisted the devil by doing what?
   a. singing hymns
   b. quoting scripture
   c. performing miracles
   d. sticking His fingers in His ears

3. The Bible says all people are tempted by the same types of things, but you can resist any temptation because God
   a. will forgive you
   b. will bless you
   c. will ignore it
   d. will show you a way to escape it

4. Jesus told His disciples they could resist temptation by watching and
   a. waiting
   b. hoping
   c. learning
   d. praying

5. What did the serpent tell Eve she would get by disobeying God in the Garden of Eden?
a. she would live forever
b. she would be like God, knowing good and evil
c. she would be beautiful and rich
d. she would be the boss over Adam

6. The Bible says money leads many people into temptation. What exactly is the problem with money?
a. having too much
b. having too little
c. loving it
d. burning it

7. When Paul and Silas were beaten and thrown into prison, they fought the temptation to moan and complain. Instead they
a. sang
b. prayed
c. cried
d. a and b

❀ ANSWERS ❀

1. b (Genesis 39:7–12)

2. b (Matthew 4:1–11)

3. d (1 Corinthians 10:13)

4. d (Matthew 26:41)

5. b (Genesis 3:1–6)

6. c (1 Timothy 6:9–10)

7. d (Acts 16:25)

154

❧ ANSWERS ❧

1. a (2 Kings 4:8)

2. c (John 19:38–40)

3. a (Ephesians 6:1–2)

4. b (Acts 10:34)

5. d (2 Kings 2:23 KJV. The kids got mauled by bears for their disrespect!)

6. b (Leviticus 19:32 KJV)

7. a (1 Timothy 5:17)

❧ QUIZ 37 ❧
RESPECT
(to show honor)

The Shunammite woman's story is about how a woman respected God's servant and was blessed for it. We don't know the woman's name. But we do know she was an important woman living in a place called Shunem.

The woman understood that Elisha was a holy man of God. She and her husband showed their respect for him by creating a little room for Elisha where the prophet could rest and be refreshed.

Elisha wanted to reward the woman for her hospitality. His servant told him the woman and her husband had no son. It seemed impossible Elisha could change this. But Elisha knew God could do anything. "At this time next year you will hold a son in your arms," Elisha told her (2 Kings 4:16). God did exactly what Elisha predicted. He gave the Shunammite woman and her husband a son.

A few years later the boy died. His mother carried him up to Elisha's room. Then she rushed to find Elisha. The woman and Elisha hurried to where the boy's body lay. Elisha shut the door and prayed, and God did another miracle—He made the boy alive again! The Shunammite woman fell down at Elisha's feet, thanking and honoring him.

Let's get some more ideas of how you can show your respect for others.

1. How did the Shunnamite woman show respect for Elisha before she built him a room to stay in?
a. she invited him to meals
b. she listened to all of his sermons
c. she donated money for his ministry
d. she shined his sandals

2. Who helped Joseph of Arimathea take Jesus' body from the cross and move it to the tomb?
a. Peter
b. James and John
c. Nicodemus
d. Zaccheus

3. In the book of Ephesians, the apostle Paul says that you are to obey and respect
a. your mom and dad
b. your Sunday school teachers
c. your sports coaches
d. your president and congress

4. The book of Acts says that God is "no respecter of persons" (KJV). In this case, this means that God
a. is so much greater, He doesn't need to respect anyone else
b. offers salvation to every person, no matter their background
c. tells people to respect themselves
d. is a respecter of animals only

5. Some youths showed disrespect to the prop. Elisha by mocking him and calling him
a. a baby
b. a yellow belly
c. a worm
d. bald head

6. According to the book of Leviticus, how should younger people show respect to the elderly?
a. by buying them groceries
b. by standing in their presence
c. by kissing their cheeks
d. by giving them a salute

7. What does the apostle Paul say good church leaders are worthy of?
a. twice as much pay
b. smiles and hugs
c. kind words and compliments
d. three weeks of vacation

RESPONSIBILITY
(your duties)

Abigail was beautiful, smart, and married to a grumpy, mean man. It was likely an arranged marriage, meaning that Abigail's father chose Nabal as her husband—probably because Nabal owned land and herds of animals. His wealth meant Abigail would be well cared for.

One day David, Israel's future king, sent his men to ask Nabal for supplies. In the past, David had been kind to Nabal, and David expected kindness in return. Instead, Nabal was rude and sent the men away. That made David so angry he came after Nabal with four hundred soldiers!

When Abigail learned of the foolish thing her husband had done, she sent her servants to David with many gifts of food and drink. Then Abigail went to David and apologized for her husband. She urged David not to react with violence to get back at him.

Abigail saved the day. But was Nabal grateful? No. When Abigail got home, she found him enjoying a feast fit for a king.

Abigail bravely stood for what she knew was right. She took responsibility for her husband's actions and put her wisdom into action.

Let's learn more about taking responsibility from these biblical examples.

1. Which of the following foods did Abigail not take to David and his soldiers?
   a. loaves of bread
   b. bottles of wine
   c. sheep prepared to eat
   d. pork chops

2. How long did it take, under Nehemiah's responsible leadership, for the walls of Jerusalem to be rebuilt?
   a. a week
   b. 52 days
   c. 3 years
   d. a decade

3. What did Mordecai tell Esther to encourage her to risk herself to save the Jews?
   a. "The Lord your God will fight for you"
   b. "Be strong and have much strength of heart"
   c. "You must not worship any other god"
   d. "Who knows if you have not become queen for such a time as this?"

4. When Naomi urged her widowed daughters-in-law, Orpah and Ruth, to return to their own people, Ruth felt it was her responsibility to
   a. leave Naomi as she'd said
   b. go live with Orpah
   c. find herself a husband
   d. stay with Naomi and help her

5. In Jesus' "parable of the talents" (or "story of the three servants and the money"), why was the third servant punished?

    a. he stole some of the money he'd been given

    b. he didn't earn as much money as the
       other two servants

    c. he didn't even try to earn more money
       with what he'd been given

    d. a and c

6. When Jesus forgave Peter for saying he didn't even know Him, what did Jesus tell Peter his responsibility would be?

    a. "Take care of My sheep"

    b. "Set up the worship tent"

    c. "Sing with joy to the Lord"

    d. "Build an ark"

7. As He hung on the cross, who did Jesus select for the responsibility of taking care of His mother, Mary?

    a. Nicodemus

    b. Mary Magdalene

    c. Peter and Andrew

    d. John

❀ ANSWERS ❀

1. d (1 Samuel 25:18. Eating pork chops
   was against God's dietary law
   for the Israelites.)

2. b (Nehemiah 6:15)

3. d (Esther 4:14)

4. d (Ruth 1:16–18)

5. c (Matthew 25:14–30)

6. a (John 21:16–17)

7. d (John 19:26–27. When he wrote,
   John called himself, "the follower
   whom [Jesus] loved.")

SACRIFICE

(the giving up of something)

Jochebed, an Israelite, had just given birth to a beautiful baby boy. Jochebed was happy but also afraid.

Pharaoh, a not-so-nice king, thought the Israelites might become powerful enough to overthrow his government. Each boy baby meant more men to fight in the future. So Pharaoh ruled that all Israelite boy babies be killed!

Jochebed hid her baby for three months, but knew she couldn't hide him forever. She put him in a basket and set it in tall grass next to the Nile River. She hoped someone would find him and save him. Jochebed's daughter, Miriam, hid near the river and watched to see what would happen.

Just then Pharaoh's daughter arrived, heard the baby cry, and felt sorry for him.

Miriam told her, "If you want to keep him, I'll find an Israelite woman to raise him until he's older," she said. Pharaoh's daughter agreed.

Miriam gave Moses back to their mother who raised her son until he was bigger. Then she gave him back to Pharaoh's daughter. That baby boy grew up to be Moses, who led the Israelites out of Egypt and freed them from Pharaoh.

Letting go of something is hard. But when you have to sacrifice something, God is right there. And He has a plan—a good one.

Here's a quiz to help you learn more about what sacrifice means.

1. What did Moses give up to become the leader of God's people, the Israelites?
   a. being known as Pharaoh's grandson
   b. the riches of Egypt
   c. the pleasures of sin
   d. all the above

2. When God told Abraham to sacrifice his son, Isaac, Abraham showed faith by preparing to do it. But God stopped Abraham from killing Isaac and provided a _____ to be sacrificed instead.
   a. donkey
   b. goat
   c. ram
   d. bull

3. Who was the first of the twelve disciples to sacrifice his life (or become a "martyr") for Jesus?
   a. Matthew
   b. Bartholomew
   c. James
   d. Andrew

4. When God accepted Abel's animal sacrifice but rejected Cain's sacrifice of fruits and vegetables, how did Cain respond?
   a. he started raising sheep
   b. he stopped making sacrifices at all
   c. he killed Abel
   d. he argued with God for hours

5. How did Jesus describe the everyday sacrifices we must make to follow Him?
   a. "take up your cross"
   b. "lay down your dreams"
   c. "put off every weight"
   d. "just say no"

6. According to the apostle Paul, why did Jesus—who was rich in heaven—become poor here on earth?
   a. to set a good example
   b. because earth money is dirty
   c. so we could become rich
   d. to make the poor feel better about themselves

7. According to Jesus, what is the greatest example of love for others?
   a. to give all your money
   b. to lay down your life
   c. to spend all your time
   d. to hand over your food

✿ ANSWERS ✿

1. d (Hebrews 11:24-26)

2. c (Genesis 22:13)

3. c (Acts 12:1-2)

4. c (Genesis 4:3-8)

5. a (Matthew 16:24)

6. c (2 Corinthians 8:9)

7. b (John 15:13)

QUIZ 40

SELF-DENIAL

(giving up your own interests and needs)

Lots of people talk about "finding yourself." The Bible talks about "denying" yourself—that is, giving up things you want for the sake of others.

Ruth Bell grew up as a missionary kid in China. She dreamed of becoming a missionary nomad in neighboring Tibet. (Nomads have no permanent home. They lead herds of farm animals to graze in fresh pastures.) Ruth's parents were missionaries in China, so she knew that being a missionary was hard work. Still, it's what she wanted to do.

But when she fell in love with a young evangelist named Billy Graham, he asked if she would marry him and give up her dream of being a missionary.

Giving up her dream to move to Tibet, China, wasn't an easy decision. Ruth prayed hard about it, and God led her to answer yes to both questions. The couple was married in 1943.

Billy wanted Ruth as his wife to support his preaching ministry. She agreed, and over many years helped Billy Graham to reach millions of people around the world with the Good News about Jesus.

Often times, God rewards our self-denial with even better things!

How much do you know about the Bible's teaching on self-denial? You're about to find out in the quiz on the next page.

1. When Jesus said, "If anyone wants to be My follower, he must give up himself and his own desires," how did He finish the statement?

    a. "he must put a lot of money in the offering plate"

    b. "he must take up his cross and follow Me"

    c. "he must pray for the strength to continue"

    d. "he must smile even when he feels like frowning"

2. What did Peter, James, and John give up to become disciples or "followers" of Jesus?

    a. a house and garage

    b. two fishing boats

    c. three bags of money

    d. everything they had

3. Jesus said, "If any man comes to Me and does not have much more love for Me than for his father and mother. . .brothers and sisters, and even his own life, he cannot be _____."

    a. My friend

    b. My son

    c. My follower

    d. My helper

4. What could Queen Esther have lost by asking King Xerxes to save her people, the Jews?

    a. her crown

    b. her reputation

    c. her life

    d. her best friend

5. What did Jesus say you should do to your hand or foot if it "causes you to stumble"—meaning, if you want to do something wrong with it?

    a. tie it down

    b. cut it off

    c. tell it to stop

    d. tattoo it

6. How did a widow in a town called Zarephath deny herself to help the prophet Elijah?

    a. she gave him the last of her food

    b. she gave him the last of her money

    c. she gave him her horse and wagon

    d. she gave him her only child

7. What does the Bible say we should "walk in" to keep from doing the things our body wants us to do?

    a. the Spirit

    b. the Ten Commandments

    c. the Psalms

    d. the Cross

❀ ANSWERS ❀

1. b (Mark 8:34)

2. d (Luke 5:11)

3. c (Luke 14:26)

4. c (Esther 4:10–11)

5. b (Matthew 18:8. Jesus probably didn't mean you should *really* cut off your hand or foot—but He wanted people to know how important it is to say no to sin!)

6. a (1 Kings 17:8–16)

7. a (Galatians 5:16 KJV)

⇒ QUIZ 41 ⇐
SERVICE
(the act of helping someone)

When Helen Roseveare studied to become a doctor, she said, "I'll go anywhere God wants me to, whatever the cost." Think about that sentence. The first part about going anywhere might cause you to imagine all the wonderful places you could go. But what about the last part, "whatever the cost"? That's the scary part. But Helen trusted God. She planned to serve Him in the Congo (in Africa) as a missionary doctor.

In the Congo, Helen worked hard, even making bricks to build small hospitals with thatched roofs where she could work to heal the sick. Her hands were torn and bleeding, but for Helen, it was worth it. Her suffering was nothing compared to what Jesus had suffered on the cross.

Within eleven years, the hospital grew to a hundred beds. Thousands of patients were helped. Helen even started clinics to serve more people. By then tired, she took a break and went home to England.

After her rest, Helen went back. She discovered things had changed. A civil war broke out. Many missionaries left. But Helen stayed. She was needed there. Nothing that could happen to her, she thought, could be worse than what Jesus had suffered.

Could you be like Helen, willing to serve God whatever the cost? Perhaps taking this next quiz can help you decide!

1. What was the "promised land" that Moses led the people toward—for forty long, hard years?
   a. Babylon
   b. Syria
   c. Galatia
   d. Canaan

2. When Naaman was stricken with leprosy, the person who told him to go see the prophet Elisha was a young girl who was serving
   a. Elisha's servant
   b. Naaman's wife
   c. Queen Esther
   d. Deborah the judge and prophetess

3. When Peter was serving God by preaching the Good News about Jesus, Herod put Peter in prison. God sent _____ who freed Peter from prison.
   a. a soldier
   b. a disciple
   c. an angel
   d. a locksmith

4. Who served the church on the island of Crete—and got a book of the Bible named for him?
   a. Titus
   b. Philemon
   c. James
   d. Epaphroditus

5. When David played his soothing harp, David was serving

    a. Elisha the prophet

    b. Saul the king

    c. Moses the leader

    d. Abraham the friend of God

6. How long did Jacob serve a man named Laban in order to marry his daughter Rachel?

    a. 2 weeks

    b. 10 months

    c. 14 years

    d. a lifetime

7. When Samuel was a boy, his mother, Hannah, dedicated him to the Lord. Samuel lived in the temple and served

    a. his mother

    b. the priest, Eli

    c. the Lord

    d. b and c

✿ ANSWERS ✿

1. d (Genesis 17:8)

2. b (2 Kings 5:2–3)

3. c (Acts 12:7)

4. a (Titus 1:4–5)

5. b (1 Samuel 16:23)

6. c (Genesis 29:26–27. Jacob said he would work seven years for Rachel, but then was tricked into marrying her sister, Leah. So he worked another seven years for Rachel.)

7. d (1 Samuel 1:12–2:11)

SINCERITY
(being real and true)

Saint Teresa of Calcutta began her life as a little girl named Agnes. Born in Macedonia to a Catholic family, Agnes longed to become a nun and work helping the poor, especially in India.

At age eighteen, Agnes traveled to Ireland where a group of nuns, the Sisters of Loretto, trained her for work as a nun in India. A new name was given to her, Sister Mary Teresa.

Sister Mary Teresa was sincere in her desire to work with the poor. She felt Jesus telling her to leave the school and work directly with the poorest of the poor. She followed His words and went into the Calcutta slums. There she nursed the sick, fed the hungry, and brought love to the lonely and forgotten. Some teachers and students she met while teaching at the convent school joined in, helping Mother Teresa with her work. As more came to volunteer, the group became known as the Missionaries of Charity.

News of Mother Teresa's work spread around the world. She received many awards, including the Nobel Peace Prize. But her most amazing honor came after her death when the Catholic Church made her a saint. Her sincerity in serving God is a shining example of how God wants you to be. If you need some tips on being sincere, look for them in the quiz that follows.

1. Jesus said that to worship God, we must worship in spirit and in _____ .
   a. soul
   b. truth
   c. purity
   d. faith

2. The apostle John urged Christians to love others "by what we do and in truth," not just by what?
   a. our thoughts
   b. our talk
   c. our sympathy
   d. our giveaway junk

3. Who said about his relationship with Jesus, "He must become more important. I must become less important"?
   a. Joseph, Mary's husband
   b. the apostle John
   c. John the Baptist
   d. "Doubting" Thomas

4. Even though Judas betrayed Him, Jesus sincerely loved Judas Iscariot. When Judas brought soldiers to arrest Him, Jesus called His disciple
   a. Dude!
   b. My child
   c. Beloved
   d. Friend

5. Jesus' sincere love for His friend Lazarus was shown by His _____ when Lazarus died.

   a. anger
   b. silence
   c. tears
   d. all the above

6. Which of these women is *not* mentioned in the Bible as someone who followed Jesus and supported Him with her money?

   a. Mary Magdalene
   b. Joanna, the wife of Chuza
   c. Susanna
   d. Jezebel

7. An Italian army captain named Cornelius sincerely believed in God. Who did God send to tell Cornelius the Good News about Jesus?

   a. Mary
   b. Philip
   c. Matthew
   d. Peter

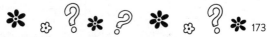

✿ ANSWERS ✿

1. b (John 4:24)

2. b (1 John 3:18)

3. c (John 3:23–30)

4. d (Matthew 26:50)

5. c (John 11:35)

6. d (Luke 8:1–3)

7. d (Acts 10:30–33)

THANKFULNESS

(feeling appreciation)

During a famine, Naomi, her husband, and two sons left Bethlehem. To find food, the family moved to Moab, about fifty miles away. Life there was good. They had food to eat, the boys grew up and married women from Moab. . .then trouble came. Naomi's husband died. Her sons died too. The only people left were her sons' wives—Orpah and Ruth.

Both Orpah and Ruth loved Naomi. They said they would move to Bethlehem to be with her. But Naomi told them to go back to their families. Orpah did, but Ruth stayed with Naomi. The two women walked back to Bethlehem.

They arrived at harvesttime. Ruth worked gathering grain in a field belonging to a man named Boaz, a relative of Naomi's husband. He was a wealthy man of God. When Boaz learned Ruth had given up her life in Moab to stay with Naomi, he acted kindly toward her.

Boaz and Ruth fell in love, and Naomi had a home with them for the rest of her life. Boaz and Ruth had a boy and Naomi thanked God for all His blessings in her life.

Naomi's story reminds us not to worry. God can take a bad situation and work it into something good. And for that, we are thankful. Perhaps you can learn more about being thankful in the quiz that follows.

1. A verse in 2 Corinthians says to give thanks to God for His amazing gift to you. That gift is
   a. salvation through Jesus
   b. good health
   c. money to live on
   d. your parents

2. According to the apostle Paul, when should Christians give thanks?
   a. each morning
   b. with every meal
   c. when times are good
   d. in everything

3. In which of Jesus' miracles did He stop beforehand and offer thanks to God the Father?
   a. the raising of Lazarus from the dead
   b. the feeding of the 5,000
   c. the healing of a demon-filled man called Many (or Legion)
   d. a and b

4. In Jesus' parable about the Pharisee and the tax collector, the Pharisee bragged about himself and said that he was thankful
   a. that he was not like other men
   b. that he went without food twice a week
   c. that he gave God a certain amount of his pay
   d. all the above

5. According to the psalms, where should we go "giving thanks"?
   a. into God's gates
   b. into all the world
   c. into the mountains
   d. into the fiery furnace

6. When the Israelites finished rebuilding the wall around Jerusalem, Nehemiah asked two large groups of _____ to lead the people in raising thanks to God.
   a. tubas
   b. singers
   c. warriors
   d. priests

7. When Jesus healed 10 men with a skin disease called leprosy, how many came back to thank Him?
   a. all 10
   b. none of them
   c. half of them
   d. only 1

✿ ANSWERS ✿

1. a (2 Corinthians 9:15)

2. d (1 Thessalonians 5:18)

3. d (John 11:1-44; Matthew 14:15-21)

4. d (Luke 18:11-12. If your prayers of thanks
      are all about how great *you* are,
         they probably aren't very good prayers.)

5. a (Psalm 100:4)

6. b (Nehemiah 12:31)

7. d (Luke 17:11-19)

≽ QUIZ 44 ≼
TRUST

(to depend on someone or something)

An angel had visited old Elizabeth's husband, Zechariah. The angel said Elizabeth would have a baby boy whom they should name John. He would be great in the sight of God, he would love God, and he would introduce Jesus to the world. Zechariah didn't believe the angel because women Elizabeth's age just didn't have babies! But Elizabeth believed. Although she didn't know God's plan, she trusted that He had one—a *good* one. She was going to have a baby!

When Mary found out about Elizabeth's baby, she hurried to visit and tell her that they both were going to have sons. What happy news! Elizabeth told Mary, "You are happy because you believed. Everything will happen as the Lord told you it would happen" (Luke 1:45). Elizabeth had faith.

Baby John arrived about six months before Jesus was born. God already had a plan for him. He would grow up to be John the Baptist, the prophet who spoke about God's Son and made people ready to meet Him.

Jesus' and John's mothers both believed what God's angel said. And both miracles happened! They were part of God's plan.

Do you trust God to have a good plan for you even when it's hard to believe? Perhaps these questions will help you build your trust in God even more.

1. Why did God give Zechariah and Elizabeth the son they longed for?
   a. they had prayed
   b. they had worked very hard for God
   c. they had given a large offering
   d. they had wept and wailed

2. Because two Jewish nurses, Shiphrah and Puah, trusted God, they disobeyed the pharaoh's order to kill Hebrew baby boys. How did God reward them?
   a. He protected them from Pharaoh's anger
   b. He honored them in the Bible
   c. He gave them families of their own
   d. all the above

3. The book of Proverbs says you are to trust in the Lord
   a. with all your money
   b. when there's no one else left to trust
   c. with all your heart
   d. when things get hard

4. Because Abraham trusted God, he believed that if he obeyed the Lord's command to sacrifice his son Isaac, God would
   a. give him another son in place of Isaac
   b. bring Isaac back from the dead
   c. immediately take Abraham to heaven with Isaac
   d. make him completely forget the experience

5. Peter's trust in God grew, and one time when Peter was in prison, God sent an angel

a. to bring him food
b. to help him write the book of 1 Peter
c. to set him free
d. all the above

6. Which king of Judah was known for his trust in God, which meant "there was no one like him among all the kings of Judah before him or after him"?

a. Manasseh
b. Rehoboam
c. Zedekiah
d. Hezekiah

7. According to the prophet Isaiah, God will keep the person who trusts in Him in perfect

a. health
b. peace
c. safety
d. cell phone reception

❧ ANSWERS ❧

1. a (Luke 1:13)

2. d (Exodus 1:15–21)

3. c (Proverbs 3:5)

4. b (Hebrews 11:17–19)

5. c (Acts 12:6–10)

6. d (2 Kings 18:5)

7. b (Isaiah 26:3)

⇒ QUIZ 45 ⇒
UNDERSTANDING
(to get the meaning of something)

Mary, Martha, and their brother, Lazarus, were Jesus' close friends. Whenever Jesus came to Bethany, He stayed with them. They knew each other well, and the three siblings trusted Jesus.

One day Lazarus became ill. His sisters worried that he might die, so they sent someone to find Jesus. They were sure that Jesus would heal their brother.

When Jesus heard, He decided to wait. He waited until He knew that Lazarus was dead! Then Jesus went to Bethany.

Mary came to meet Him with tears streaming down her face. She didn't understand why Jesus hadn't come earlier and healed her brother. When Jesus saw how sad His friend was, He cried too. Jesus understood her pain. But He had a good reason to wait until Lazarus died. Jesus was about to prove to disbelievers in Bethany that He truly was God's Son.

He went with the sisters to Lazarus's tomb. Many of the villagers came too. Then Jesus prayed, and in a loud voice He cried, "Lazarus, come out!" And out came Lazarus, alive and perfectly well. The villagers ran to tell others what Jesus did. Then Mary understood why Jesus had waited to come.

You may not always understand why God is doing what He does but God understands—and He wants you to trust him. Let's see just how much you understand in the questions following.

1. At first Mary and her sister Martha didn't understand why Jesus had let their brother Lazarus die instead of healing him. What did Jesus tell them?

    a. Lazarus was better off in heaven now

    b. Lazarus's death would allow Jesus to show God's shining-greatness (or glory)

    c. Mary and Martha needed to rely more on themselves

    d. the twelve disciples would step up to care for Mary and Martha

2. Jesus said He spoke in picture stories (or parables) so that some people would understand and others wouldn't. What was the difference in people's ability to understand?

    a. some had much more education

    b. some were born with bigger brains

    c. some people just didn't care

    d. God shared His secrets with certain people

3. According to the Proverbs, people of understanding

    a. keep quiet

    b. win favor

    c. are slow to get angry

    d. all the above

4. Who prayed by saying, "I ask God to fill you with the wisdom and understanding the Holy Spirit gives"?

    a. Jesus

    b. Daniel

    c. Priscilla and Aquila

    d. Paul

5. Who told Egypt's Pharaoh to "look for a man who is wise and understanding" to prepare the land for a time when food would be scarce?

a. Pharaoh's baker
b. Benjamin
c. Pharaoh's cup-carrier
d. Joseph

6. Because God gave Daniel knowledge and understanding, he was able to

a. interpret dreams
b. organize the king's banquets
c. translate the record of Babylon into Hebrew
d. prescribe medicine

7. According to the apostle Paul, where are all the "riches of wisdom and understanding" hidden?

a. in the ark of the covenant
b. in scripture
c. in Christ
d. in Mesopotamia

❀ ANSWERS ❀

1. b (John 11:38–40)

2. d (Matthew 13:10–12)

3. d (Proverbs 11:12; 13:15; 14:29)

4. d (Colossians 1:1–9)

5. d (Genesis 41:33–40)

6. a (Daniel 5:12)

7. c (Colossians 2:3)

VIRTUE

(goodness; knowing right from wrong)

When Jesus hung dying on the cross, He said, "Father, forgive them. They do not know what they are doing" (Luke 23:34). As a Christian, Betty Olsen knew those words, and she likely remembered them in her final hours on earth.

Betty wanted to be a missionary nurse. She went to nursing school. Then, in 1964, she received an assignment to serve in a missionary hospital in Vietnam.

The country was in the middle of a deadly war. Betty's family and friends worried about her going, but Betty felt at peace with her assignment. She decided that even if she didn't come back, as many soldiers hadn't, she was carrying out God's will for her. Betty believed Vietnam was where she should be.

Several years into her assignment, the enemy raided the military hospital. They captured Betty along with two men. The prisoners were treated horribly—put in cages, starved, beaten, and made to walk for miles. Only one man survived. Later he told the story of Betty's bravery and selflessness. "She never showed any bitterness or resentment," he said. "To the end, she loved the ones who mistreated her."

Betty's story tells the true meaning of courage and forgiveness, two of the many virtues God wants us to show in our lives. Discover more about virtues in the following quiz.

1. The Golden Rule which says, "Do for other people whatever you would like to have them do for you" can be found in which of the following books of the Bible?

    a. Genesis

    b. Psalms

    c. Matthew

    d. 2 John

2. The apostle Paul urged Christians to always think about things that are

    a. true and respected

    b. right and pure

    c. lovely and well thought of

    d. all the above

3. The book of Proverbs says that a virtuous woman (or a good wife) is worth far more than

    a. gold

    b. rubies

    c. diamond

    d. gourmet jelly beans

4. The apostle Paul told the people who lived in Colosse to be compassionate, kind, and forgiving, and over all of those virtues to put on _____ which holds everything together perfectly.

    a. peace

    b. love

    c. honesty

    d. faith

5. In the book of Galatians, the virtues of "love, joy, peace, not giving up, being kind, being good, having faith, being gentle, and being the boss over our own desires" are known as

　　a. the virtues of Jesus
　　b. the signs of discipleship
　　c. the gifts of the heaven
　　d. the fruit of the Spirit

6. What important Bible woman heard an angel tell her, "You are honored very much. You are a favored woman. The Lord is with you. You are chosen from among many women."

　　a. Miriam
　　b. Deborah
　　c. Mary
　　d. Mary Magdalene

7. When God told the ancient Israelites that they should have "a full and fair weight," what did He mean?

　　a. too much dieting was not virtuous
　　b. they should be honest when they bought
　　　 and sold things
　　c. offerings to the temple should be heavy
　　d. wrestling matches should include guys
　　　 in the same weight class

✿ ANSWERS ✿

1. c (Matthew 7:12)

2. d (Philippians 4:8)

3. b (Proverbs 31:10)

4. b (Colossians 3:12-14)

5. d (Galatians 5:22-23)

6. c (Luke 1:26-28)

7. b (Deuteronomy 25:13-16)

❧ QUIZ 47 ❧
WAITING
(being patient)

Hannah and Peninnah were Elkanah's wives. (In those days, men often had more than one wife.) Peninnah enjoyed bullying Hannah because Peninnah had children and Hannah didn't. The bullying made Hannah very sad, but instead of talking back or doing something else to make the situation even worse, she took her trouble to God.

Hannah went to the temple and prayed, asking God for a son. She promised that if God gave her a son, she would give the boy back to Him. She would allow him to be raised in the temple so he would grow up to serve God.

God answered Hannah's prayer! He gave her a son. She named him Samuel, which means "asked of God." And Hannah kept her promise. When Samuel was old enough, she took him to the temple and asked Eli the priest to raise him and teach him to serve God. God blessed Hannah with five more children. And Peninnah? The Bible says nothing more about the bully.

If someone hurts your feelings, be like Hannah. Tell God. He loves you. Then wait patiently for God to do what's best for you.

Let's see what else God's Word has to say about the waiting game.

1. While Hannah was waiting to see if she would ever have a child, she
   a. cried really hard
   b. prayed to God
   c. got bullied
   d. all the above

2. The book of Lamentations says that people who wait on the Lord will find that He is
   a. good
   b. generous
   c. powerful
   d. pleased

3. After His resurrection but before He returned to heaven, Jesus told the disciples to wait in Jerusalem for what?
   a. His second coming
   b. the prophecy of Daniel
   c. the Holy Spirit's arrival
   d. the conversion of Saul

4. What Old Testament character, who suffered terribly, is described in the New Testament as patient?
   a. Jephthah
   b. Job
   c. Jeremiah
   d. Jonah

5. The book of psalms says we should wait _____ for the Lord to do what He says He will do.
   a. busily
   b. excitedly
   c. patiently
   d. manfully

6. Because Abraham was willing to wait for God, what did he get?
   a. a Mediterranean cruise
   b. flocks and herds
   c. an angel visit
   d. God's promise

7. According to the book of 2 Corinthians, what is one thing you should *never* wait to do?
   a. be saved
   b. start exercising
   c. read good books
   d. tell your mom you love her

✿ ANSWERS ✿

1. d (1 Samuel 1:7, 10)

2. a (Lamentations 3:25. But God is all of those other things too!)

3. c (Acts 1:4–5)

4. b (James 5:11 KJV)

5. c (Psalm 37:7 KJV)

6. d (Hebrews 6:13–15)

7. a (2 Corinthians 6:2)

⇝ QUIZ 48 ⇜
WORK
(a job to do)

God put the idea in Emeline Dryer's heart to teach others about Jesus. Emma wanted to obey God. So she left college and set out to do His work.

Emma moved to Chicago where she met a preacher, D. L. Moody, who spoke to large crowds, teaching them about Jesus. Mr. Moody admired Emma's teaching skills and her strong Christian faith. He encouraged her to start a training school for missionaries. It would be the missionaries' jobs to go to the homes of people who didn't know Jesus and tell about Him.

With Emma in charge, the school grew. Many learned to love Jesus. Then those people taught their children about Jesus and raised them to be Christian men and women.

Emma died at an old age in 1925, still serving God. Her school, Moody Bible Institute, continues to exist in Chicago, training others to do God's work. Emma gave up everything to help God work His plan. She was left with not a lot of money, but she always had enough to live a good, happy life.

We learn from her story that when we choose to do the work God gives us to do, He gives us exactly what we need.

Now let's see how good a job you do working on the quiz questions!

1. After Adam ate the forbidden fruit of the tree of the knowledge of good and evil, God told him that now he would have to work hard
   a. growing his own food
   b. breaking rocks in a quarry
   c. keeping the animals from fighting
   d. picking up apples in the fall

2. The Bible says you are to do your work with all your heart. And to do it for the Lord and not for
   a. the money
   b. fame
   c. the king
   d. men

3. In Egypt Joseph first worked for Potiphar, then a jailer, and then Pharaoh. Joseph did well in whatever work he did because God
   a. was with him
   b. showed him kindness
   c. gave Him favor
   d. all the above

4. While Nehemiah was helping to rebuild the walls of Jerusalem, he did his work with one hand and in his other hand he held
   a. a drink
   b. a weapon for protection
   c. a scroll of scripture
   d. a picture of his wife

5. On the seventh day of creation, God ended His work, then
   a. rested
   b. tested
   c. jested
   d. nested

6. To keep them from starving, Naomi told Ruth she should work in a nearby field
   a. planting flowers
   b. pulling weeds
   c. picking grapes
   d. gathering up leftover grain

7. What did Jesus promise to everyone whose work was heavy and tiring, if they came to Him?
   a. a helper to cut the load in half
   b. angels to take over
   c. a cool drink of water
   d. rest

❁ ANSWERS ❁

1. a (Genesis 3:17–19. The work itself wasn't a punishment—Adam had worked before. But after sin was in the world, the work was a chore, not a joy.)

2. d (Colossians 3:23–24)

3. d (Genesis 39:20–23)

4. b (Nehemiah 4:17)

5. a (Genesis 2:2–3)

6. d (Ruth 2:2)

7. d. (Matthew 11:28)

⇒ QUIZ 49 ⇐
YEARNING
(wishing hard for something)

Betty Scott was an American whose parents were missionaries in China. While attending school in America, Betty planned to return to China and become a missionary. One day she wrote, "I want something really worthwhile to live for. . . . I want it to be God's choice for me and not my own."

Betty met her future husband, John Stam, while they were students at Moody Bible Institute in Chicago. During her college years, Betty felt God calling her to serve in Africa; but John planned to travel to China to do mission work. Through it all, Betty trusted God to lead her in the right direction. And He did!

It soon became clear that God had different plans for Betty. He wanted her to move to China! Although John had one year of schooling left, Betty decided she would leave for China. At that time, the couple wasn't engaged. The following year, John traveled to China and reunited with Betty. The couple married after they returned to China to do mission work.

When you have a yearning to do what God wants you to do, He will make it happen. Let's see what more God wants to teach you about yearning in this quiz.

1. Jacob's wife Rachel yearned to have a child. After a long time, God finally blessed her with a son she named
   a. Joseph
   b. Jacob Jr.
   c. Jesse
   d. John

2. Jesus knew that when He ascended to heaven His disciples would miss Him and yearn to see Him. So the disciples were promised that Jesus would
   a. one day see them in heaven
   b. come back again some day
   c. visit them in their dreams
   d. hear and answer their prayers

3. What did a psalm writer say his soul yearned for—that he wanted so much he became weak?
   a. to be in the Lord's house
   b. to find peace on earth
   c. to build a house of cedar
   d. to teach the world to sing

4. Haman yearned to kill Mordecai and all the Jews but instead Haman ended up
   a. having to honor Mordecai
   b. killed on the tower he built to hang Mordecai
   c. working in the king's stable
   d. a and b

5. David's son, Absalom, yearned to be king instead of his father, so Absalom
   a. told the people that he cared about them more than David
   b. gathered an army to fight his father
   c. declared himself king
   d. all the above

6. Zechariah and Elizabeth yearned to have a child, but when an angel told the old priest he would have a son, Zechariah didn't believe him. So the angel
   a. made Zechariah unable to speak until his son was born
   b. lifted Zechariah up to heaven
   c. sadly told Zechariah he had little faith
   d. blinded Zechariah with a flash of lightning

7. What does the book of Proverbs say a fulfilled yearning (or longing or desire) is?
   a. lucky for you
   b. the first step to success
   c. sweet to the soul
   d. something to be proud of

✿ ANSWERS ✿

1. a (Genesis 30:22–24)

2. b (Acts 1:9–11)

3. a (Psalm 84:2)

4. d (Esther 6:10; 7:9–10)

5. d (2 Samuel 15:4, 10; 17:1–3. These bad
   yearnings ended up getting
   Absalom killed.)

6. a (Luke 1:19–20)

7. c (Proverbs 13:19)

ZEAL

(excitement or passion for something)

Lottie Moon loved Jesus and wanted to work in China as a missionary, but it was unusual then for unmarried women to serve as missionaries overseas. Still, God made it possible for Lottie to go.

In China, where few people believed in Jesus, Lottie found it difficult to encourage them to accept Christ as their Savior. She discovered that first she needed to be their friend and *show* them, instead of *tell* them, how to be Christians. She moved to a small village in the Chinese countryside and tried to be friendly with people there. Often she baked cookies. When children smelled the delicious treats baking, they went to her house, and before long Lottie met their mothers. As she made friends, the people began listening to her stories about Jesus, and many accepted Him into their hearts.

Maybe you know people who need Jesus. You're not too young or too small to make a difference, to have a passion. Be like Lottie. Set a good example. Ask God to help you lead them to Christ.

Now let's see how much zeal some other people had for God.

1. Through the prophet Haggai, God scolded the Israelites because their zeal was to _____ instead of repairing and rebuilding His temple.

    a. build houses for themselves

    b. buy and sell cattle

    c. organize sporting events

    d. mine for gold

2. When evil men plotted against Daniel, he showed his zeal for God by

    a. mocking the evil men

    b. preaching on the street corners

    c. copying scrolls of scripture by hand

    d. praying three times a day

3. What did Daniel say would happen to people who were wise and zealous to "lead many to do what is right and good"?

    a. they would have songs written about them

    b. they would make the world a happier place

    c. they would shine like the stars forever

    d. they would appear on TV

4. After meeting Jesus at the well, an excited Samaritan woman went into town, telling them to go see Jesus. She asked them, "Could this be _____?"

    a. Moses come back to earth

    b. the man to overthrow Rome

    c. the Christ

    d. our new governor

5. What Old Testament prophet, who defeated 450 prophets of the false god Baal, said he had been very zealous for the Lord God?

    a. Elijah

    b. Micah

    c. Isaiah

    d. Zechariah

6. The church in Laodicea had lost its zeal, and Jesus said He didn't like the people's "lukewarm" ways. What did He threaten to do with them?

    a. light a fire under them

    b. cast them into a snowbank

    c. shine the light of the sun on their works

    d. spit them out of His mouth

7. Jesus told the people in Laodicea that His strong words were spoken in love. What did He want them to do to regain their zeal for Him?

    a. be sorry for their sins and turn from them

    b. pray without ceasing

    c. sell all they had to give to the poor

    d. memorize 200 Bible verses

✿ ANSWERS ✿

1. a (Haggai 1:2–9)

2. d (Daniel 6:10)

3. c (Daniel 12:3)

4. c (John 4:29)

5. a (1 Kings 19:10)

6. d (Revelation 3:15–16)

7. a (Revelation 3:19)